FIRE
UPON THE EARTH

The Story of the Christian Church
By NORMAN F. LANGFORD

Illustrated by John Lear
Cover illustration by Drew Thurston

D080242

Sonlight Curriculum Ltd.

This edition published 2001 by Sonlight Curriculum, Ltd., upon Payment of royalties to and by permission of Westminster Press.

Printed in the United States of America

For a catalog of Sonlight Curriculum materials for the home School, write:

Sonlight Curriculum, Ltd.
8042 S. Grant Way
Littleton, CO 80122-2705
USA

Or e-mail: catalog@sonlight.com

CONTENTS

$\mathcal{P}art$ I

THE CHURCH CONQUERS
AN EMPIRE

CHAPTER 1

TWO EMPIRES

O N a couch of gold and ivory stood a wax image of Augustus Caesar, conqueror of his world, founder and ruler of the Roman Empire.

Below the couch with its image Augustus himself lay resting, as quiet as his statue. The name of Caesar he had borrowed from his illustrious great-uncle, Julius Caesar. From now on, all future emperors of Rome would take it for a title. But no mortal ruler had ever before been called Augustus—"The Majestic." It was a title for a god.

The lands he governed circled the Great Sea, the Mediterranean. Far countries that had long been cursed by war were now at peace, because Augustus Caesar had conquered them. His legions patrolled the frontiers, ever on guard against invasion from the barbarous folk that lived beyond. No nation was at war with any other, for the majestic emperor ruled them all. Roadways built to carry Roman armies also carried the wealth of the civilized world, as merchants traveled safely across the Empire. Ships laden with rich cargo sailed the Mediterranean. Where the Roman governors ruled, men counted on justice being done.

Full of gratitude, the assembly of the province of Asia had once framed a greeting for the birthday of Augustus:

> This day has changed the earth. The providence which rules over all has filled this man with such gifts for the salvation of the world as to make him the savior for us and for coming generations. Of wars he will make an end. . . . It is impossible that one greater than he can ever appear. The birthday of God has brought to the world glad tidings.

In all the cities of Asia, it was ordered, this greeting should be inscribed.

Now the image on the couch stared with unseeing eyes of wax; and the eyes of the great man himself were sightless too, for death had put out the light. Below the couch, Augustus Caesar lay in his imperial coffin.

All Rome turned out to watch the funeral. Crowds thronged the streets, or climbed to the housetops under the hot September sun, to see Augustus take his last journey through the streets of the city he had made so beautiful and great. An image of Augustus, made of gold, was carried behind the coffin; and with it were images of his ancestors and of famous Romans of other days.

The procession paused by the temple built in honor of Julius Caesar. There a tall, gaunt man named Tiberius, destined to be the successor of Augustus, delivered a speech. He praised the virtues that the late emperor had loved and practiced: his devotion to his country, his generosity, his frankness, his gifts as a ruler. The oration over, the procession moved slowly on until the dome of the Imperial Mausoleum came into view. The body of Augustus was laid on the funeral pile, and at a signal centurions applied their torches. The flames leaped up, and at the same instant an eagle was released to fly upward into the boundless sky—a sign that the soul of Augustus had soared to heaven. The ashes were laid in the huge round mausoleum among the cypress trees.

Soon afterward the Roman senate met, and decreed that Augustus Caesar was now one of the gods of Rome.

In the provinces of the Empire there was sorrow that so

great a benefactor was gone. But as a god he still might help and save his people. While he was yet alive, the Eastern folk who loved to make gods out of their heroes had paid him divine honors. Now that he was sublime in death, great cities would compete in building temples worthy of his name. And not only Augustus but the Caesars after him who sat upon his throne would find themselves hailed as gods.

There were gods and goddesses enough already. The imagination awoke at the very mention of their names: Hecate, Queen of the Night; Infernal Proserpine; Queen Isis of Egypt; Zeus, and Mars, and Saturn. Perhaps, some said, these were but different names for one great god. But there was room for another—one whom all the nations of the Empire should unite in worshiping.

"Hail, Caesar." There was power in that name. Sweet odor of incense drifted heavenward, while loyal knees from East to West bowed low.

About fifteen years after the death of Caesar the Majestic, in a remote part of the Empire another man died and was buried under very different circumstances.

It was in the time of Pontius Pilate, the Roman governor of Judea, who could have wanted nothing less than to get involved in a dispute among the Jews. Who could understand a stubborn nation that insisted on calling itself "the chosen people" and classing all other nations together under the uncomplimentary name of "Gentiles"? There was scarcely a city in the Empire without a settlement of Jews; and everywhere they lived to themselves and followed the religion of their fathers, a riddle to everyone except those few Gentiles—the so-called "God-fearers"—who attended the synagogue. It was Pilate's luck to be made governor of the Jewish homeland; and now, sitting in court at Jerusalem, he had to come to a decision about a case that baffled him.

The local authorities had brought him a prisoner named Jesus, demanding that the death sentence be passed upon this man. Pilate's Roman sense of justice told him that the accused was innocent of any crime. It was not even clear to him just what the prisoner was charged with. Evidently Jesus had claimed to be "a son of the gods," as Pilate understood it.

A feeling of uneasiness passed over Pilate. After all, there were such things as gods. The Jews, however, did not seem to think so. They taught that God is invisible; and the story went around that they worshiped a spirit in an empty box. The government did not greatly care what they worshiped, so long as they paid their taxes and kept the peace. Rome had given them a license, as it had all other nations, to practice their own religion. Why could they not settle their disputes among themselves?

The Jewish authorities were loudly declaring that Jesus had been guilty of blasphemy, and ought to die. Something was also said about his claiming to be "King of the Jews." That was more in Pilate's line. The government had to be careful about rebellions against Rome, and one never knew when the Jews would revolt. They did not share the general gratitude to Caesar.

A glance at Jesus reassured Pilate. The man was quite alone, his own followers having deserted him. A glance at the crowd, however, shook the governor's confidence. There was surely danger of a riot, if Pilate refused to do as he was asked.

The safest course seemed to be to pass the death sentence. But this would scarcely be equal to the standards of Roman justice. With a feeling of disgust, Pilate uttered the fatal words: "Take him, and crucify him. I wash my hands of this whole affair!"

Thus it was that Jesus was led out, with two thieves who also had to be put out of the way just then, and nailed up on a cross. It was the most degrading punishment known, reserved for the lowest and most dangerous type of criminal.

When evening came, a wealthy friend quietly removed the body of Jesus from the cross. Under the cover of night he laid it in a tomb in a garden. A stone was rolled against the door.

Seven weeks later, the city of Jerusalem was crowded with Jewish visitors from many lands who were attending the festival of Pentecost. At about nine o'clock in the morning there was a commotion. A sound like rushing wind was heard, and, stranger still, the sound of voices speaking in every language known to the visitors present at the scene. A crowd soon gathered where the disturbance was taking place, and observed that the voices were those of twelve men standing in a group.

"What has happened now?" everyone wanted to know. "And how is it that each of us hears those men speaking in his own language?"

Someone laughed. "The fellows are drunk!"

The voice of Peter, a former fisherman and a disciple of Jesus, rang out:

"Everyone at Jerusalem, listen to my words! God has sent his Holy Spirit to speak to you. God is among you! He sent Jesus of Nazareth, and you killed him. But death could not hold him prisoner—such a thing was impossible. God raised him from the dead, and we ourselves saw it. We, his disciples, are the witnesses! Let all Jews know this: God has made this Jesus, whom you crucified, your Lord and your Messiah!"

Peter waited for the response. It came in the cry of many voices: "What shall we do?"

"Turn from your sins," Peter answered, "and be baptized in the name of Jesus, so that your sins may be forgiven. Then the power of God will enter into you. Save yourselves while there is time!"

As though they had heard God speak from heaven, three thousand people believed Peter's words. They were baptized, and joined the disciples. They listened to every word the disciples had to say. From that day they prayed together and ate in one another's homes; praying and eating together, they felt the presence of One who had died and broken out of the grave. The power that can raise the dead was alive among them, and a strength greater than their own lifted them up from the death of sin. They shared their belongings. They sold their possessions and brought the price to the disciples, so that it might be given to the poor.

The three thousand soon became five thousand. The new

faith was talked of in private homes and where men gathered at the Temple. Leaders must be chosen. Seven men were elected as deacons, to look after the needy. Still more believed; and wherever the believers went, the people of Jerusalem stopped to look and listen.

The Jewish authorities at Jerusalem were alarmed. A new faith had sprung up almost overnight, and it was out of control already. The rulers threatened the disciples. When that failed, they whipped them. Finally, there came an outburst of fury and Stephen—one of the seven deacons, and the first man to die for having faith in Jesus Christ—was done to death.

It was a mistake. The believers fled from Jerusalem, where prison bars, and lashes, and perhaps death itself, awaited them. But when they fled, they took their faith along, and wherever they went they spoke of it. It was soon the talk of Palestine. Instead of stamping out the new belief, the rulers had spread it throughout the country.

But it was only the Jewish authorities who were disturbed. The Roman government took no part in the affair. Pilate had washed his hands of the matter, and did not interfere again.

Meanwhile, on the rocky and romantic island of Capri, off the coast of Italy, the aging Tiberius Caesar had set up his home. From there he ruled the world around the Mediterranean Sea. No trifling rumors from far-off Judea would reach him there, nor would he be likely to worry about them if they did. He had commanded his armies for a long time, and he knew how secure the Roman Empire was—more secure even than when Augustus died.

A cold, suspicious man, more feared than loved, Tiberius ruled the world he knew; and he ruled it efficiently and well. He had had mutinies to deal with, and he had put them down by force. A new religion in Judea was not a thing to trouble him.

Even in Jerusalem, the Romans did not take the new religion seriously. "There seems to be a new kind of Jew," they thought. And they had long since given up trying to understand the Jews.

CHAPTER 2

MEMOIRS OF AN APOSTLE

THE ship turned off from the Mediterranean, and steered inland along the Cydnus River toward Tarsus. To one of the passengers, a young Jew named Paul, home and safety lay ahead.

Paul stared into the river. It was an ugly stream, but no native of Tarsus could gaze at it without pride. The engineers of that enterprising city had dug its channel deep and wide. The gateway to one of the wealthy provinces of Asia Minor, Tarsus was now also a port of call for the great ships. Rich cargoes passed in and out of its harbor, and men of many races mingled in its streets.

Among those bustling crowds Paul might lose himself if he chose. There had been enemies in Jerusalem who had tried to murder him, but they would hardly follow him this far. It was not that Paul had been afraid—after his encounter with a power that was more than human, why should he fear the weapons of men? But his friends had had no peace of mind until they had hurried him from Jerusalem to the seacoast and had set him on a ship for home.

Home! It had been with high hopes and young ambition

that Paul set out from home some years before. The whole world lay before him then, for Paul had been born a Roman citizen, free to travel where he would throughout the Empire. The Greek he had learned to speak at Tarsus would make him understood wherever he might wish to go. One place, however, had called to him above all others: Jerusalem, built amid desolate hills, remote from the busy city where he had been brought up. For Paul was determined to be a teacher of the Jewish faith; and Jerusalem, with its schools and learned rabbis, was the fountain of the knowledge for which he was so thirsty.

He had proved himself a brilliant student and a fierce defender of the faith of his fathers. When the scandal about the crucified carpenter broke out, how eagerly Paul joined in the hunt for followers of Jesus! To fight against these blasphemers was to him a sacred duty. Jerusalem alone was not large enough to contain the holy fury that seized him. He would go to Damascus too, and smash, wreck, demolish the uprising there; he would not come back from Damascus without new victims as his prisoners.

Then as he neared Damascus there had come a fierce and sudden light that knocked him to the ground like a physical blow. There had come the unearthly voice, "I am Jesus whom thou persecutest."

And now Paul was coming home to Tarsus. He was eager to preach Christ Jesus—more eager even than he had been to oppose him—but it was not clear to him what he ought to do. Would he ever live down his reputation as a persecutor? Would the followers of Christ ever accept their old enemy as a friend and ally? There were deep-seated suspicions to be overcome, memories of the terror and dismay that the very name of Paul used to strike into the hearts of Christ's believers. And there was also the enmity of the men who had once been Paul's intimates, and who now hated him as a traitor—a hatred so ferocious that Paul had barely escaped from Jerusalem with his life.

Paul looked at the crowd waiting for the ship to come in.

Perhaps here, in the Jewish settlement within Tarsus, he might spread the gospel. But what the future held for him, he could not yet foresee.

The ship put in to port. Paul went ashore, and disappeared up one of the city streets.

Some twenty years after that landing in Tarsus, another ship—the *Dioscuri*—was making its way along the coast line of Italy, passing the island of Capri. The chief mission of the ship was to bring a load of corn from Egypt to feed Italian mouths. It also happened that a Jew named Paul was aboard, bound for Rome to appeal to Caesar himself to be cleared of the charges that Jewish enemies had laid against him.

As the *Dioscuri* swung into the lovely Bay of Naples, the splendor of an Italian spring lay upon the land. The beauty of the morning seemed to welcome Paul to the country he had so long yearned to visit. His boyhood in Tarsus had taught him to see the vast horizons of the Roman Empire, uniting all the ancient world. Many a time he had dreamed of going to Rome itself, the capital and hub of the immense dominion.

Soon he would reach his goal. He had been born and bred a city man, and soon he would be in the greatest city of them all. Paul's memory roamed again through the other cities he had visited in his long career. He remembered how his travels had begun, when the good apostle Barnabas had sought him out in Tarsus. He had not been forgotten after all! There was work for him to do in places far from Tarsus. Barnabas came to take him to Antioch in Syria. It was at Antioch that the first large congregation of Gentiles was formed, and the Jerusalem leaders hardly knew what to do with it. Barnabas had thought of Paul as a likely man to help, for Paul had been brought up in a Gentile city. For a whole year the two men worked in the congregation at Antioch. The population of the city heard that some new god named Christ was being worshiped there, and invented a nickname for his worshipers—"Christians."

From Antioch in Syria, Paul and Barnabas had been sent out as missionaries. Paul recalled how they traveled through a mountainous wilderness, a land of lonely places and wild tribes and highway robbers, until they reached another Antioch—Pisidian Antioch, as it was called. He would not forget that city, for there he had reached a new turning point in his life. As was their custom, Paul and Barnabas preached in the synagogue, announcing that the Messiah had come. The Jews received their message coldly. But in the congregation were Gentile "God-fearers," who, although not Jews themselves, found inspiration in the synagogue services.

"Come again next Sabbath," the God-fearers implored, "and preach to us once more."

When the next Sabbath came, almost the whole city turned out to listen to the service. The Jews were jealous, and began to contradict the preachers. Paul and Barnabas came to a great decision. Addressing the Jews, they said:

"Because you are the people of Israel, it was our duty to preach to you first. We had to tell you that your Savior has come. But you have thrust the truth away from you. You have proved yourselves unworthy of eternal life. Therefore—we turn instead to the Gentiles."

Back in Jerusalem, however, the Christian leaders were uneasy about the way the Gentiles were streaming into the church. Was it right to treat Jews and Gentiles as though they were the same? Was it possible to become a Christian except by first becoming a Jew?

Paul remembered the great council held at Jerusalem to discuss this very question. He himself had said little on that occasion, leaving it to the older leaders, such as Peter and James, to make the decision. A compromise was agreed upon. Certain of the simpler Jewish laws must be obeyed by Gentile Christians, and nothing further would be asked of them. As for Paul and Barnabas, it was decided that they should be missionaries to the Gentiles. Their sacrifices and successes had proved them suited to the task. Other apostles should continue to preach to the Jews.

After this, Paul had had a freer hand. He was clear in his own mind about the attitude he ought to take. Becoming a

Christian did not mean becoming a Jew. It meant becoming free—free from sin, free from death, free from all differences of race or nation. Before Christ all men were equal, all were sinners, all were offered pardon. "There is no difference," Paul wrote, "between Jew and Greek: the same Lord is Lord of all."

Paul's memory carried him back to places where he had stood long years before. He recalled setting his feet upon the shore of Greece. He had made history on that occasion. That was the time when, in obedience to a vision he had by night, he crossed from Asia, taking the gospel to Europe. He thought of Philippi, the first city in Greece where he had preached. He thought of it warmly, for no church was dearer to him than the one in that place. When he had time, he must write a letter to the Philippians. Perhaps he loved that church all the more because of the suffering it had cost him to establish it. He could see the face of the mad girl whom he cured of her insanity. He could recall the angry faces of the girl's masters, who had sold her services as a fortuneteller, when they found she was of no more use to them. He could hear the shouting of the mob against himself and his companion Silas when word went around that they were disturbing the city. He could shut his eyes and feel the bitter sting of the whip, the blood springing from his back and the sweat standing on his forehead, when the magistrate had the preachers flogged.

More pleasant memories slipped into his mind. He felt his feet once more on the marble tiles of the road south from Philippi; he heard the wind in the trees, and tasted the sweet water of the wells bubbling up from mountain streams. He saw in his mind's eye the view from Thessalonica, across the bay to the snow-capped hills. He pictured the Roman legions, their gold standards gleaming in the noonday sun as they marched along the imperial road which ran through Thessalonica, and the rocky hills around the city, blood red in the sunset. There was the howling of a mob to face there also— a sound to which he would become accustomed in his travels. He could hear the shouting: "The men who have turned the world upside down have come here! They preach that there is another king besides Caesar, another king named Jesus!" But most of all he remembered that at Thessalonica too there was a church that would remember him, for he had founded it.

Once more, in memory, he stood in Athens, where the greatest artists and thinkers of olden time had lived and worked. Beautiful temples to the gods adorned the city. People said that he had come to preach a new god, Jesus. And when he told his curious listeners that Jesus had risen from the dead, no one laid a hand on him. The audience laughed instead.

Then there was Corinth, the greatest port of Greece, standing midway in the Empire, full of sailors and businessmen and agents of the government. The very rich lived there, and beside them lived the very poor. Luxury abounded there, and such vice and evil also that the very word "Corinth" stood for filthiness. For a year and a half Paul labored there, winning a few of the rich and many of the poor to Christ. In that wealthy and wicked city, even Christians had got drunk at the Lord's Supper. When Paul left Corinth, the church split up into parties, fighting each against the other. Yet, Paul reflected, it was still the church of Jesus Christ. The Lord would redeem his people, and not abandon them to their sins.

There was Ephesus to remember too—Ephesus, back in Asia. There stood the temple to the goddess Artemis, whom the Romans called Diana—a temple that was one of the wonders of the world. Who could forget the clamor that broke loose when the silversmiths found that the people who believed Paul's message no longer bought the little idols that they made and sold? A mob was stirred up to a frenzy. The city itself had been insulted by this insult to its goddess. For two solid hours the crowd stood chanting: "Great is Artemis of the Ephesians!" This was another time, Paul recollected, that he owed his life to his friends. He had wanted to go to address the mob, which would have torn him limb from limb, but his friends had held him back.

And now the ship was nearly into port. It had been a long life's journey, through many cities and many countries and across deep waters, to reach the land of Rome itself.

There had been floggings and stonings, mobs and robbers, hunger and thirst, loneliness and shipwreck. Such was the life of an apostle—one of those wandering missionaries who had seen Jesus in his lifetime or seen him in vision, and whose task it was to carry the gospel far and wide. The trials had not been merely sufferings of the body. It was a heavy care and a great responsibility to be leader of so many churches spread across so vast an area. The little congregations did not yet possess sufficient leaders of their own: they must look to the apostles, such as Paul, to encourage and to guide them. And if the honor given to the apostle was great, great also were his burdens.

Yet Paul had had good friends to work with him. Amid so many hardships, his life had been long preserved. The Roman power had often protected him: for Rome stood for justice, and Paul was a Roman citizen. To many it seemed that Paul was only preaching some new god—and that was harmless, for there were many gods already. To the government it seemed that the Church was only a branch of the Jewish faith—and the Jews were left to settle their own affairs.

It was the Jews—his own countrymen—who had caused Paul most of his trouble. Again and again they had accused him of disturbing the peace; and there was always the danger that the Roman courts would finally decide that it was safer to do away with Paul. That was why, after this last arrest, he had decided to appeal to Caesar.

Paul was the enemy whom the Jewish authorities chiefly wanted to destroy. At Jerusalem, the Church was not often molested any more; it was doing little harm. Had men only foreseen it, Jerusalem itself would before many years be wiped out by a Roman army, and the Church would be scattered from the place where it began.

But Paul had spread the new faith across the Empire. In city after city, a new church had risen up. Some of the Jews had believed Paul's message, but not enough to make much difference. It was mainly Gentiles who had flocked after him. Not from among the Jewish people, but from among the "heathen," the support of the Christian Church had chiefly come.

Paul could look back with thankfulness. His letters were being read in churches throughout the Roman Empire. Someday, though he did not know it, they would be gathered together with the Gospels and other writings not yet written, to form the New Testament.

But now the *Dioscuri* was in harbor, and Paul was ashore. Enough of looking back! There was Rome to look forward to— the place where he had longed to be.

From the port where Paul disembarked it was about 130 miles to Rome. Halfway there, he was overjoyed to be met by Christians from the capital, who had walked so many miles to meet him. Their warm greetings drowned out the little clicking sound that accompanied Paul's every step along the road.

The sound was that of a chain, binding Paul arm to arm with a Roman officer. For Paul was going to Rome indeed — but as a prisoner.

For two years he lived and preached in the greatest of cities, under guard by day and night. And what then was done with him, or where his body lies, is a secret no man knows.

CHAPTER 3

YES OR NO?

EVEN with slaves to guard their treasures, the rich of ancient Rome slept badly. They feared the alarm in the night, the dreaded cry of "Fire!" But who would wake the poor, in the third or fourth stories of the flimsy apartment houses, before the flames crept up the wooden beams to roast them in their beds alive?

Fire was the bad dream of every Roman. And every day bad dreams came true, and someone's house was reduced to smoldering ruins. Not many years after Paul had gone to Rome the crowded city woke to find that the worst of nightmares was not so bad as what was really happening. It was the night of July 18, A.D. 64. Usually so dark, the capital was already bright before the sun had risen. Men were shouting; children shrieked; women screamed. A fire was out of hand! All Rome was burning!

The pitiful supply of water was of no avail against the flames. Across the narrow streets sparks blew back and forth, kindling fresh fires in every quarter of the city. This was only the beginning. For ten long days of terror the blaze burned on, as though the whole of Rome were doomed to perish. People trampled one another underfoot, fleeing from the flames. Some went mad and threw themselves into the fire. Others died trying to rescue their possessions.

When the fire had spent itself at last, there rose a bitter cry from the ashes. Someone must be to blame for the calamity! Rumors spread as fast as the fire had done.

"Haven't you heard? There were people hindering the fire fighters!"

"Worse than that—they started new fires everywhere in the city."

"Somebody must have paid them. And you know who it was."

"Yes, of course! Our fat, nearsighted emperor—Caesar himself!"

"Well, it's just the kind of thing you would expect him to do. He likes music and dancing better than attending to his business. Did you know that he has filled his palace with actors and jockeys and zither players?"

"Yes, and they say he started the fire to enjoy a good show! Now he's going to build Rome better than it was before. That was part of his plan!"

So ran the common talk. The fat Caesar, Nero, probably never thought of burning Rome. It was one crime of which he was innocent. But a Caesar who had murdered his mother was not a man who found it easy to defend his good name. The only way to escape suspicion was to blame the fire on someone else. "Who," he asked himself, "who else is despised and hated in the streets of Rome?"

There was only one answer. The Christians, to be sure!

That is why, on the charge of burning Rome, great numbers of Christians were put to death. Some were beheaded and some were crucified. Some were covered with the hides of wild beasts and worried to death by dogs. At night Nero made a brilliant pageant in his gardens: the light was provided by Christians, burned alive to serve as human torches. Before he had finished with the Christians, there were even some of the Roman people who were moved with pity for the sufferers.

Perhaps there were some who doubted whether the Christians were guilty after all. But that did not matter greatly. For, as an ancient writer explained, it was not so much because they had really set the fire that they were punished. It was because they were "enemies of the human race."

Wherever Romans had learned to tell the difference between Jews and Christians, all through the Empire, that was the opinion of the man in the street: Christians were enemies of the human race. Because they were already so much hated, Nero could put the guilt of the fire upon them. Who would rise to their defense?

The pagan could not understand what it was that the Church was standing for; but he saw what it stood against. The Christian was against the races, the games, the gladiatorial shows; against the spectacle of slaves fighting in the arena for their lives, or of criminals thrown among wild beasts; against the amusements, and brutal sports, without which the crowds thought they could not bear to live. Some of the more enthusiastic Christians went farther, and said that to enjoy oneself was sin; and for the extreme words of the few the many were blamed. The Christians, it was said, were against everything: they were enemies of the human race.

The Christians were against the practice of leaving infants out to die on the city garbage heap. The pagan father thought his child belonged to him; and if, because the infant was a girl or for some other reason, he did not wish the child to live, the baby's life was at his mercy. The Church taught that every person's life is precious in the sight of God; that God gave life, and to God belongs the right to take life away.

What, then, if the father were a pagan, and the mother a Christian? Or what if the father were converted, and, to his wife's disgust, gave away money for Christian charity? What if a daughter turned Christian, and refused to marry the man her parents had chosen for her because he was a pagan? Many times, the people of a neighborhood first learned of Christianity when they saw that it had broken up a home. Their first thought was: "The Church is the enemy of homes."

Most of all, the Christians were against the idols, the superstitions, the false gods of their pagan neighbors. Some went to the length of defacing the images and tearing down the idols. None would take part in the gay, wild festivals in which the gods and goddesses were worshiped. None would make a sacrifice on Caesar's name day, and say, "Lord Caesar," calling on the Roman emperor as a god. So it was said, "The Church is the enemy of religion."

Where was the God of the Christians? people asked. Who had ever seen him? The Christians must be against all gods. They must be atheists—and "atheists" became the name by which they were known. It was abominable, men thought, to insult the gods. More than that, it was dangerous. Floods, storms, earthquakes, famines, plagues—all were sent by the gods. It was, men declared, the atheism of the Christians that had angered the gods, and made them send such curses on the earth. Let a flood come, let an epidemic break out, let there be a drought—and some Christian might have to die for it.

Enemies of the human race: and popular talk went farther, and said that the Christians were murderers. "Do you know what they are doing behind their closed doors? They eat babies!" Cannibals! Could anyone be so vile?

Thus the hatred spread, and the wild tales with it. What was going on in the meetings of the Christians—still held in private homes, for there were no church buildings yet— was very different from anything that the pagans imagined. The Christians had no day, no Sunday, on which they were free from work. Therefore they rose very early once a week—or more often—to meet before their working hours began. Together they read the Old Testament; or perhaps some precious letter from one of the apostles, or at a later date a passage from the Gospels. Someone with a gift for it explained the scripture, as in the Jewish synagogue. Together they sang psalms or hymns. A leader led in prayer, while the rest responded "Alleluia," or, "Thanks be to God." Or perhaps several prayed in an outburst of ecstasy. Those who spoke said nothing of any crimes they meant to do. Their advice to one another was not to ruin homes. They preached that workers should be industrious, that husbands and wives should be faithful to one another, that all should be honest and truthful and law-abiding. They prayed for help that they might do those good things which the gospel taught them.

Finally, they ate and drank together. Bread and wine were on the table; and before they partook of it they gave adoring praise to God, and remembered Christ's work on earth, and called on the Holy Spirit to bless what they were about to do. Then they took the bread and wine, believing that the body and blood of the Lord Jesus were present.

In some neighboring house the word perhaps was whispered, "The cannibals are eating flesh again!"

Or it might be that they gathered at the close of day, their labor over, tired from work, but not too weary to worship God and talk together for a while. It was a "love feast"—as they called it—for which they assembled at the evening hour. First they prayed, and then the lamps were lighted. Each would be asked to sing, either a hymn from scripture or one of his own composing. They read letters from distant churches, and encouraged one another. Someone might have brought a basket of good food to share with the rest, or to be given to the needy. The meeting ended, as it had begun, with prayer. But what dark deeds their neighbors imagined they had been planning, under cover of the night!

Yet there were some who came to understand the truth. There were many won to the new faith: had there not been so many, the Church would not have been so much hated. Again and again it happened that some pagan who came to the Christian meeting place to sneer or to satisfy his curiosity remained as a new member of the Church. When they learned what the gospel was, many were convinced that their idols, and all the heathen gods and goddesses, were nothing; that the one true God was he who had come to earth in his Son Christ Jesus.

If they could not see this God, they saw the deeds of love that he inspired. They saw that Christians welcomed all who

21

came; that among them slaves had as honored a place as rich men. They saw how they cared for one another, and each with the other shared what he had, while the poor were given food and clothing and kindness where Christians were. "See how these Christians love one another!" one man exclaimed.

Yet rumor still had it that they were cannibals. "Away with the atheists!" cried the mob. And it was generally agreed that whether they committed any crimes or not Christians hated all mankind.

What happened to the Christians depended on how their neighbors felt about them, and on the mood of the Roman governor in the place where they were living. They could not go to court and plead for justice, for they had no rights in Roman law. To be a Christian was automatically a crime. Other religions were given official permission to exist and were thus made legal. The Church was an illegal faith. It was therefore in the power of the government to arrest a Christian and punish him whenever it saw fit.

In the first two hundred years it seldom happened that the government took action against the Church. Nero had done it, for his own purposes; but there were later emperors who were wiser and more just. They preferred to let Christians live in peace, so long as there was no great outcry against them. It was ordered that no one should be punished merely because another person accused him of belonging to the Church. Too many pagans were suffering because their enemies had blackened their names by calling them "Christians"! So serious a charge must be proved before a man might be condemned!

Always, however, the danger hung over Christian heads: at any moment the government might act. Many a Roman governor must have been tempted to use his power against the Church. For, like every government that conquers a vast empire and rules it by force, the Romans feared secret societies among the people. Was this illegal brotherhood called the Church really loyal to the Empire —especially since its members refused to swear by Caesar as a god?

Besides, the Church was beginning to be well organized —it was too much like an empire within the Empire. In the early days, the apostles who traveled from place to place held the highest authority in the Church. Local affairs in the congregations were managed by the presbyters —the "older men" who had proved their worth. As the apostles died off, each congregation looked to its own bishop. To him was given the honor formerly given to apostles; on his shoulders rested more and more the duty of ruling the local church. The more the churches suffered, the more they looked for leadership to the bishop. And the more solidly the Christians stood together behind their leaders, the worse the danger seemed to the Roman government. Moreover, since the government treated the Church as a secret society, Christians were driven more and more to meet in secrecy. Under Rome, and other cities, they laid their dead in great caves and galleries; and amid these underground tombs they met for services, or to find refuge from persecution. But the government feared that any group that met in secret might be hatching schemes against the Empire.

Nevertheless, the Roman government, in these first two centuries, did not desire to make things hard for the Christians. Whenever public feeling would explode in a riot against the Christians, the governor in that place would bring the accused before the court. It was very easy for them to leave the court free and unharmed. Each was asked a single question: "Are you a Christian?" If the accused said, "No," he was released, perhaps being required to prove himself sincere by making a sacrifice to the gods and saying, "Lord Caesar." If he said, "Yes," the patient governor might ask him over and over again, hoping that he would at last come to his senses and deny the charge. If he persisted in admitting that he was a Christian, he might be jailed or fined. He might be beheaded, or he might be put to death by torture. He might be thrown to the wild beasts in the arena, to make sport for a Roman holiday. It all hung upon a simple "Yes" or "No."

The government made it easy to escape, without many

questions asked. And because it was so easy to escape, and so terrible to remain behind for the punishment, the choice was hard. Jesus had said: "Whosoever therefore shall confess me before men, him will I confess also before my Father which is in heaven. But whosoever shall deny me before men, him will I also deny before my Father which is in heaven." The Christians found that this meant to confess or deny, not merely in private or before a friendly congregation, but before a judge and court of law. To say, "I confess to being a Christian," was to confess to a crime. To deny—that was the way out, always held open. Many must have taken it, and made it harder for the rest, who confessed and remained to die.

Many, however, found that, when they had to choose, the easy thing was after all to tell the truth. The bishops set a good example. There was Ignatius, the great bishop of Antioch. He was accused of the capital offense of being a Christian. Friends would have intervened to save him, and that was what he feared most of all. He dreaded, not to be thrown among wild beasts, but to be saved by any help but God's. This is the message that he sent:

> I write to all the churches and charge them to know that I die willingly for God, if you hinder not.... Let me belong to the wild beasts, that I may reach God. I am God's grain, and I am ground by the teeth of wild beasts, that I may be found pure bread.

He had his wish. And the night after the animals tore him to pieces, his friends dreamed they saw him. They seemed to see him dripping with sweat, as if he had just finished a work of great labor. Polycarp, bishop of Smyrna, was such another. Although an old man, he would do nothing to save himself from the flames. When the fire that consumed him was at last burned out, the people of his congregation rescued his bones from the ashes—counting them more precious than diamonds or gold.

The honors did not belong to leaders alone. As slaves had sat beside rich folk at the love feasts, so they took their place among bishops in the ranks of the martyrs. The mob had its way with a slave girl named Blandina, upon whom every kind of torture was inflicted. Yet it was she who won the contest, for no agony could induce her to say anything except, "I am a Christian, and there is no wickedness done amongst us." They made her watch her brother die: a boy of fifteen, who took courage from his sister's example, and suffered torture and gave up his life rather than swear by the idols of the heathen. Blandina herself was whipped, placed upon a roasting chair, tied in a net, and gored to death by a bull. Then she had peace at last, and with a good conscience, because she confessed Christ Jesus.

These were called "wrestlers," who wrestled against the temptation to deny their Lord. These were hailed as the "athletes" of the Church, who ran a good race and won the crown of victory. The more they were put to shame and suffering by the anger of the pagans, the more they were honored by all who believed in Christ. How many there were, no one knows. If there was any danger, it was not that too few would confess and die, but that too many would come forward to earn a martyr's fame even when there was no need for them to suffer.

Brave wrestlers and good athletes, they triumphed through a strength greater than their own. Asked if they were Christians, they said, "Yes," and died. And because they died, the Church of Christ lived on.

CHAPTER 4

ROME AGAINST GOD

THE Emperor Decius was a man with high ideals and many problems.

At the far eastern edge of the Empire, Persian armies were in combat with the soldiers of Caesar. But that was only one of the problems. From the north and the east, hordes of tall, warlike men were moving down from the great forests, to press against the Roman borders. These were the Goths, the ancestors of the German people. To the civilized Romans, they were just "barbarians." Calling them barbarians, however, was not going to keep them out of the Empire. That was a job for an army—and a better army than the Empire possessed. By the year 249, when Decius ascended the throne, one could no longer count upon the once-proud legions of Rome to hold their own against foreign invaders. Besides, it took money to support the armies on the far-reaching frontiers, and the citizens of the Empire were growing poor. Then, as if the emperor had not anxieties enough already, the dreaded pestilence broke out.

To Decius it seemed that his real problem was not the Per-

27

sians in the east or the Goths in the north. It was not armies and it was not taxes; neither was it the plague. There was one great problem which included all the others: that was how to recapture the spirit of ancient Rome. Being a high-minded man, the emperor looked back and sighed for days gone by. He longed for the pure religion and the clean living that his imagination pictured in the Rome of olden times.

There was an enemy within the borders, Decius thought —a fifth column, a traitorous company which had corrupted the glories of the Empire. The Christian Church had betrayed the religion of ancient Rome.

In the year 250, Decius issued an imperial edict. On a certain day it would be the duty of every governor, of every magistrate, to see that no one failed to do his religious duty. On that day, everyone within the Roman borders must sacrifice to the gods and to Caesar.

It came as a shock to the Christian Church. Almost fifty years before, there had been an imperial decree forbidding Jews and Christians to spread their faiths. But the trouble had soon blown over, and for nearly half a century now the Church had grown and prospered peacefully. The great centers of empire—Alexandria in Egypt, Antioch in Syria, Carthage in North Africa, Rome itself—had also become great centers of Christianity. Christian scholars had written books, professors had lectured on Christian doctrine without anyone interfering with them; conferences of Church leaders met in East and West. No longer was it necessary to hold services in private homes alone: the Church could afford to have its own buildings for sacred use, with the Holy Table set apart, behind which the bishop presided over his increasing flock. Seldom did ignorant mobs seek to stir up riots. No more was it said that Christians were atheists and cannibals. The Church had earned the respect of the common people, and in growing numbers they were being won to the Christian faith.

But Decius said the Church must go. Decius had his ideals. He would restore the old religion throughout the Empire, and in that way make Rome great again. It was not that he sought the death of any Christian. All he asked was that Christians should give up their faith. If they should disobey, there would of course be torture and prison—even the death penalty when extreme cases might require it. But how much better it would be if only the Christians would co-operate; if only they would turn back, and share the emperor's dream!

The shock was too much for many of the Christians, unaccustomed for so many years to persecution. Some actually sacrificed to the gods to escape the punishment. Others bribed officials to let them slip by the altar without making the sacrifice required. Still others bought from the magistrates certificates which declared that they were faithful pagans:

> I have always sacrificed regularly to the gods, and now, in your presence, in accordance with the edict, I have sacrificed, and poured the drink offering, and tasted of the sacrifices, and I request you to certify the same. Farewell.
>
> Handed in by me.
>
> . . . . (signature of applicant)
>
> I certify that I saw him sacrificing.
>
> . . . . (signature of magistrate).

Later they would have to answer to their fellow Christians for these perjured papers. The Church indeed scarcely knew what to do with those who had proved so weak in the day of testing. The sterner Christians would have refused them admission back into the Church. Others thought that any who were genuinely repentant were worthy of a second chance. The decision finally was that where "the lapsed," as they were called, had a reasonable excuse, and repented of their shame, they might publicly confess their fault and at last return to the ranks of the Church. Even lapsed ministers might be received again into the fellowship—though nevermore to do the work of the ministry.

At all events, the cowardice of the lapsed brought no new glories to the Roman Empire, and the Church as a whole was steadfast. The weaklings were quickly weeded out, and the strong stood their ground. Decius was forced to confess defeat in his first attempt to break the Church; and he had no opportunity to try again, for soon afterward he died in battle against the Goths. For a time no one knew who was emperor, and a fresh epidemic of the plague added to the confusion and horror of the times. The Christians, having shown their courage when their faith was threatened, lived up to their faith when the pestilence attacked. Pagans might often flee from the deadly sickness, leaving their own relatives to suffer and to die. The Christians stayed to nurse the sick, to ease the suffering, and to bury the dead, making no distinction between pagan or Christian, friend or foe.

Yet their services were badly rewarded when Valerian shortly became emperor. The new Caesar issued orders more savage than Decius had dreamed of. Those who met for Christian worship were subject to the death penalty. All clergymen were to be put to death and could not save themselves even by giving up their faith. Leaders other than clergymen were allowed to live, but only if they renounced the Church. Wealthy Christians were to be deprived of their property. It was Valerian's plan that if the Church survived at all, it would have none but the poor and destitute for members.

Valerian himself, however, had not long to live. The Persians captured him, and he died a prisoner. Valerian's son, Gallienus, now ruled at Rome, and by his orders the property of Christians was restored to them. He did more than that. Places of worship were given back to the Church, and now for the first time in history Christians might legally gather for worship.

Another wave of persecution had come and gone. The Roman government itself had tried to destroy the Church; and yet the Church still stood. Peace—peace at last— seemed to lie ahead.

When Diocletian became emperor, in the year 284, the most imposing building in the Eastern city of Nicomedia was a Christian church. Diocletian could not have failed to see it, for it was Nicomedia that he made his capital. It was his opinion that the place for the supreme ruler of the Roman Empire was not in the West, not in Rome, but in the East: near the frontiers where the barbarian hordes were forever pressing against the imperial troops.

If the prominence of the Church in Nicomedia annoyed Diocletian, he gave no sign of it at first. So widespread had Christianity become that it was now well established even within the emperor's palace. Diocletian himself remained a pagan, but his wife and daughter studied to become Church members.

This great and able ruler was for long too occupied with reorganizing the Empire to concern himself with religion. The Empire, he believed, was too large for one man to govern well. Calling himself Augustus, and making his capital in the East, he also appointed another Augustus to rule the West. Each Augustus had a Caesar to assist him. For the first time in many years the Empire was governed efficiently. Even the invaders from beyond the frontiers were held in check.

As the years went on, the exertions and worries of his work began to tell upon the emperor. His health was breaking under the strain. His nerves were cracking up. Ugly suspicions took root in his mind. His son-in-law, Galerius, perhaps took advantage of the opportunity to pour warnings and advice into the emperor's ears: "Don't you see what is at the bottom of all our troubles? Don't you realize that it is the Christian Church which has made the Empire so weak? Your duty is to stamp out the Church!"

Diocletian was slow to act upon his son-in-law's advice. Yet—what if Galerius were right? Doubt and fear took hold of him. At last he could no longer resist the constant urging. The storm broke on February 23, 303.

From the imperial palace came the order that all Christian churches were to be destroyed. All copies of the scriptures were to be burned. Christians of high social rank were to lose their citizenship. Others would be reduced to slavery.

Galerius was not satisfied. He longed for bloodshed, but Diocletian was not ready to go so far. yet it was bad enough;

and in Nicomedia itself the great church was destroyed by imperial troops. Diocletian might have done nothing further if two fires within two weeks had not broken out in the palace. As in Nero's day, the Christians were blamed. Diocletian issued another order: All clergymen were to be put in prison.

The prisons were quickly filled, and Diocletian tried to empty them by offering freedom to all who would return to the pagan religion of the Empire. When that failed, a desperate order was decreed, forcing Christians to make their choice. Either they would sacrifice to the gods or they would die.

Soon afterward Diocletian resigned from the burdens of his office. Those who took over his power threw away all restraint. The full fury of hatred against the Christian Church was let loose. In one city alone, an observer watched a procession of almost a hundred Christians on their way to slave labor in the mines: a pitiful procession of broken bodies, men, women, and children, their right eyes put out, their left feet crippled with hot irons. Prisons were full. In some towns fragments of bodies were strewn around the market place.

Special care was taken to discover all copies of the scriptures and destroy them. To try to save one copy was to suffer the death penalty. In Sicily a Christian was brought before the governor, on the charge of possessing a copy of the Gospels.

"Where did these come from?" asked the judge, pointing to the books. "Did you bring them from your home?"

"I have no home," replied the prisoner, "as my Lord Jesus knows."

Once again pointing to the Gospels, the judge said, "Read them!"

The Christian opened the Gospels, and read, "Blessed are they which are persecuted for righteousness' sake: for theirs is the kingdom of heaven."

He turned to another place, and read again, "If any man will come after me, let him deny himself, and take up his cross, and follow me."

The prisoner was led away to torture and to death. In his agony he cried out, "Thanks be to Christ my God!"

Never before had the Church faced so fierce an onslaught. The Christians were unarmed. The Empire had all its power to throw against them. The Church could defend itself in one way only, and that was by dying. It was the defense, however, and not the attack that succeeded. The government at length, after eight dreadful years, acknowledged its own defeat. Galerius upon his deathbed, being a superstitious man, grew afraid. His own gods had failed him. Perhaps the God of the Christians might save him now!

Galerius issued a decree ordering the persecution to cease. He had, he confessed, been mistaken; and he besought the Christians that they would pray for him.

Thousands had died, or been put to the torture. Never knowing when violent death might come upon them, men dreamed much of another world than this. They comforted one another with the thought of the beauty and the peace that lay ahead. "Angels," it was said, "would carry them eastward, past the storehouse of hail and snow, past the fountains of rain, past the spirits of wickedness which are in the air, and carry them to the seventh circle, setting them down full opposite the glory of God."

All who suffered knew that this trouble was but a passing incident: the Church would live on forever. "When Diocletian was emperor," men would say, to give the date of an event. And Christians added, "In the reign of the Eternal King!"

For all the Christians knew, persecution might come again. There were many rivals for the emperor's throne, and who could tell whether a friend or an enemy would eventually gain it?

In the West an ambitious man named Constantine was fighting his way toward the headship of the Empire. In the year 312, as he prepared for battle with a rival, the story is told that he saw against the evening sky a vision. He saw a cross of light; and with it were the words, "In this sign conquer."

That was the inspiration that Constantine needed. Other emperors had tried to make the Empire strong by destroying the Church. But one twentieth of the population was Christian now, and that was too large a number to destroy. Besides, the Church grew stronger and not weaker through suffering. It was Diocletian himself who said, "As a rule, the Christians are only too happy to die." And a Christian leader wrote, "The blood of martyrs is the seed of the Church."

Constantine decided upon a new policy. He would strengthen the Empire, not by attacking the Church, but by befriending it. The Church had proved itself, in nearly three centuries of testing. Constantine could tell which was the winning side, and that was the side to be on. "In this sign conquer."

Constantine won his battle, the day after the vision. The next year he and a partner met at Milan in Italy, and sent out this message: "We have seen that we have no right to refuse freedom of religion. To see to matters of belief must be left to the judgment and desire of each individual, according to the man's own free will." Perhaps now the Christian God would bless Constantine and the dominion that he ruled!

Ten years later Constantine was supreme ruler of the whole Roman Empire. Until this time he had been satisfied to let all religions be equal. Now, however, although the pagan religions were not suppressed, Constantine's laws began to favor Christianity. Sunday was set aside as a weekly holiday. Officials were no longer required to make sacrifices to the gods: which meant that Christians could at last hold public office in the Empire. Part of the taxes were given to the Church, as had

formerly been done for the pagan priests. Children were protected as they never had been before. Even the animals in the postal service benefited, for drivers were forbidden to be cruel to their horses.

The great change had come. Constantine set up a new capital at the old city of Byzantium, and named it after himself: Constantinople. In the center of the city stood a Christian church. A few years later visitors marveled to hear how the Passion of Christ was depicted, at the palace, in precious stones. Or they stood before the statue of Constantine, and read the inscription on the column: "O Christ, Ruler and Maker of the world, to thee have I now consecrated this obedient city and this scepter and the power of Rome. Guard and deliver it from every harm."

Constantine being emperor, in the reign of the Eternal King, it came about that Christians in the Roman Empire need never more fear the torture seat, the fury of the persecutor, the wrath of angry Caesar.

CHAPTER 5

ESTABLISHING THE GAINS

THE evening silence was broken by the sound of a boat cutting its way through the waters of the Nile. Bishop Athanasius of Alexandria shrank back into the shadows along the bank. That would be the police.

Someone must have caught sight of him in spite of the darkness. A voice called out, "Have you seen Athanasius?"

"Yes," the fugitive coolly replied; "you are not far from him now."

The boat sped on its way up the river. Athanasius moved quickly in the opposite direction, disappearing from sight before the searchers should discover their mistake.

His enemies would stop at nothing to overthrow him; but he could be as resourceful as they. Once they had charged him with causing a disturbance at the Lord's Supper, so that the cup was broken and the consecrated wine was spilled. Athanasius proved that there was no church in the village where the disturbance was supposed to have happened. Another time he was accused of murdering a man, and cutting off his hand to use it for working magic. Athanasius produced the man in court: alive, and with both his hands.

He had always been a fighter. It had been with a determined spirit that he set out for Nicaea, some years earlier, in the year 325, to attend the council of the Church which the emperor Constantine had summoned in that Asia Minor town. Athanasius was a very young man then, and not yet a bishop. But he had been privileged to sit with the three hundred leaders whose task it was to settle the dispute which was splitting the Church in two.

Most of the older delegates had in their earlier years been in prison for their faith, and many of them bore scars. One had lost an eye during the persecution. Another had lost the use of his hands under the torture. But the days of suffering seemed over now. They did not set out secretly, as they used to do, fearing arrest. They did not painfully walk the long miles as once they did. They rode in comfort to Nicaea, all their expenses paid, the guests of the emperor.

As the young Athanasius traveled on that memorable journey, his ears had rung with the catchy verses, the popular songs, that then were being sung in the streets of Alexandria. Why, one had only to visit the wharves to hear workmen humming the ditties as they loaded fish! Arius had been clever, putting his ideas into witty rhymes, setting them to pleasing tunes. But Athanasius had gone to Nicaea, filled with a great resolve to defeat Arius in the debates.

Arius was a minister in Alexandria of Egypt. He taught that Christ is a creature halfway between God and man.

He was more than human, Arius said, but less than God. Once, according to this teaching, God lived alone, and had no Son. Then he created Christ, who in turn created everything else that is. The idea appealed to many of the former pagans, for it was so much like the religion in which they had been brought up. The old pagan religion taught that there is one supreme God, who dwells alone, and then a number of lesser beings, who do God's work and pass back and forth between heaven and earth. Converts from paganism found it hard to grasp the Christian belief that Christ has always existed from all eternity, and that he is equal with the Father. Arius made

Christianity easier to understand. It seemed more reasonable to think of Christ as a kind of divine hero: greater than an ordinary human being, but of a lower rank than the eternal God.

What was the use, Athanasius thought, of having won the struggle with the pagan Empire, if pagan ideas were going to be taught in the name of the Church? So many martyrs had suffered and died for the sake of the Lord Jesus Christ. And now Arius and his followers seemed to be saying: "This Jesus Christ is not quite what the Church has thought he is. You have to look higher than Christ if you want to find God."

The emperor also had been concerned about the dispute, though for a different reason. Constantine was counting on the Church to bring new life into a weary Empire. But only a strong Church would be of use to him. A divided, quarreling Church would be more of a hindrance than a help. Constantine was not so much interested in the truth: what he wanted above all was to keep the Church united.

That was an unforgettable day—July 4, 325—when the delegates seated themselves in the conference hall at Nicaea, and waited for their host to arrive. In the center of the room was a chair, and a table on which lay an open copy of the Gospels. Presently a tall man in a purple silk robe strode in. The purple marked him as the head of the Roman Empire, Constantine himself. But, unlike his usual practice, he entered without any train of soldiers. As a sign of respect for the Church Fathers, he had left his military guard behind.

Constantine spoke briefly. He told his hearers that they must come to some agreement on the questions that divided them. Division in the Church, he said, was worse than war. Having thus spoken, he stepped aside. The meeting was in the hands of the Church leaders.

There were of course many at the council who were ready to compromise. They would have agreed on any statement that left everyone free to think as he liked. But Athanasius was not of those. He and the others who were against Arius kept insisting: "We must think clearly. We must come to a decision."

In the end Arius and his supporters were voted down. A creed, a statement of belief, was issued, which no Arian could accept. In part it ran:

> We believe in one God, the Almighty Father, creator of all things visible and invisible.
>
> And in one Lord Jesus Christ, the son of God, who alone was begotten of the Father, that is of the substance of the Father, God of God, Light of Light, very God of very God....
>
> And in the Holy Ghost.

All but two bishops present signed the creed; and these two, along with Arius himself, were soon afterward sent into exile. Meanwhile Constantine was joyful, thinking the issue settled. He held a great banquet, at which the head of the Empire and the bishops of the Church sat down together and celebrated the coming of happy days to the Church of Christ. Bishop Paphnutius, who had lost one eye under the emperor Diocletian, was singled out for special honor by the new emperor. As a sign of friendship between the Empire and the Church, Constantine kissed the bishop's eyeless cheek.

But if the Arian dispute could have been so quickly settled, Athanasius would not have been hiding from police boats on the river Nile. Three years after the Council of Nicaea, Athanasius became bishop of Alexandria, and that was when his struggle with the Arians really began. Book after book came from his pen: he never wearied of defending the faith of the Church against the teachings of Arius. But it was not in peace and security that he wrote his books. Throughout the Eastern part of the Empire, the quarrel raged on: the Church could not agree on who Christ really was. There was brawling in the streets, riots and bloodshed. Worshipers at divine service tried to shout each other down. Above all, there was constant court intrigue, with leaders on both sides of the dispute seeking to gain the favor of the emperor. As the chief defender of the Church's faith, Athanasius was the chief victim of the plotting. Five times he was banished from his post, and forced to flee. The saying arose: "Athanasius against the world!"

For fifty years it remained uncertain who would win the battle. It could have happened that the Church would accept the belief in Christ as someone who was neither God nor man. But it turned out that Athanasius was not after all alone against the world. He lived to see the triumph of the cause he championed. When he died at the age of seventy-five, his death was peaceful. He had been at last secure in his office as bishop of Alexandria in the closing years, and—what mattered more to him—he could rest assured that the creed he had fought for at Nicaea and ever afterward was the creed of the Church.

The doctrine of the Holy Trinity had come to stay. "Jesus Christ . . . God of God, Light of Light, very God of very God." Athanasius had taken part in the writing of the creed. And one year after Athanasius died, there came to the bishopric of Milan, in faraway Italy, a great man named Ambrose who had a skill in writing hymns. Across the long miles of land and sea, Athanasius could have joined Ambrose in better verses than Arius wrote:

> O splendor of God's glory bright,
> O thou that bringest light from light,
> O Light of light, light's living spring,
> O Day, all days illumining.

> O thou true Sun, on us thy glance
> Let fall in royal radiance,
> The Spirit's sanctifying beam
> Upon our earthly senses stream....

> All laud to God the Father be,
> All praise, eternal Son, to thee;
> All glory, as is ever meet,
> To God the holy Paraclete.

It was this same Ambrose who proved once and for all who had won the war between the Empire and the Church.

Ambrose had never intended to be a clergyman at all. His father was a devoted Christian, but he had found his career in the service of the Empire. He had, in fact, become one of the four highest officials in the province of Gaul, which now is France. Young Ambrose was trained to follow in his father's footsteps. After studying the law, he entered the emperor's service and was put in charge of a province, with his headquarters in the city of Milan;

The bishop of Milan at that time was a follower of Arius, and the people of the city were glad when he died. Yet they were afraid that others would die before a new bishop was elected: for the Arians would want another of their own kind appointed, and the election might lead to rioting and bloodshed.

On the day of the election Governor Ambrose went to the cathedral. The clergymen of the city were there, and so were a great crowd of the people. Nervous excitement ran through the whole assembly. Suddenly the thin, clear voice of a child cried out:

"Ambrose for bishop!"

That was the solution! The cathedral rang with demands for the governor to become bishop of the Church. In vain did Ambrose protest that he had no training or talent for the post. Why, he had not even been baptized! Like many another person in his day, he had postponed baptism, for there was a fear in men's hearts of punishment for sins committed after one had taken the baptismal vows. But neither the clergy nor the people would be refused. In the end Ambrose had to accept the honor, and the emperor gave his approval. In eight short days the governor was baptized as a Christian, ordained a priest, and consecrated a bishop.

The gifts that had made him a governor so young stood him in good stead now that he was head of the Church in Milan. He had been trained in oratory, and his magnificent sermons were the talk of the city. He knew how to govern and he ruled the Church like a statesman. Toward the Arians he was unyielding; yet when the Arians lost the struggle, he saved many of them—even his personal enemies—from exile and suffering. To the poor and the humble he was always kind. Of the high and the great he was never afraid.

In the year 390 shocking news came to his ears. The emperor Theodosius had been angered by the city of Thessalonica because an imperial governor had been murdered in a riot there. This place, said the emperor, would be made an example to all the world. Fitting punishment would be visited on the city that had done violence to a representative of the emperor, to a servant of the majestic Augustus!

The fatal order was given: all the people of Thessalonica were to be put to death.

It was not carried out to the full. But the gates were closed, and for three hours of horror the soldiers were busy with their swords. When at last the command was issued to cease the massacre, seven thousand of the trapped population had been slaughtered.

Feeling himself avenged, Theodosius returned to his residence in Milan. Like a faithful Christian, it was his intention to attend divine service in the cathedral.

He was met at the door of the church by Bishop Ambrose. But the bishop had not come out to do honor to the emperor.

"Go away," said Ambrose—"go away, until you are ready to confess your sin and do penance for it!" And he would not conduct the service if Theodosius was present in the church.

For nine months the emperor held out. During that time he stayed away from all worship, bitterly complaining of how he had been used.

"The Church of God," he said, "is open to slaves and beggars. To me it is closed, and with it the gates of heaven!"

Powerful ministers of state begged Ambrose to yield. But Ambrose remembered the seven thousand victims of Thessalonica. Not even the imperial purple of Theodosius, not the title of Augustus, would gain the emperor admittance to the cathedral of Milan before he had repented of his sin.

At last Theodosius came again to the door of the church. This time he did not demand to be admitted. Lying prostrate on the floor, the ruler of the Roman Empire confessed his sin and implored forgiveness.

Now Ambrose was ready to receive him back into the Church. The emperor could once more take Communion. Even yet, however, he had not understood his proper place.

Theodosius strode to the front of the cathedral, and mounted the chancel steps to present his offering at the altar. He was met by the hand of Ambrose—not stretched out in greeting, but raised in a signal to come no farther.

"The purple," said Ambrose, "makes emperors, not priests."

Humbly Theodosius retired among the worshipers.

The man who had first borne the majestic name of Augustus had been called a god.

Theodosius also took the title of Augustus. But in the Church this Augustus was only one of the people. In the Church the bishop ruled alone.

$\mathcal{P}art$ II

THE CHURCH BECOMES
AN EMPIRE

CHAPTER 6

THE CHURCH TAKES OVER

A CLOUD of dust, rolling ever nearer, arose on the South Russian plain. If it were only the wind, all was well. The people of the village strained their eyes anxiously, searching for the cause. It was as they feared. The dust was raised by the hoofs of swift little horses, ridden by yellow men—short, hairless men—armed with bows and arrows. The Huns had come.

It would be over quickly. Wherever the bands of these cruel marauders rode, there was slaughter. Once the Huns had been the curse of China. The Chinese finally drove them from their borders, and the Huns turned westward. Across the vast stretches of Asia they rolled on, raiding the countryside wherever they went, killing the unlucky inhabitants who crossed their path. At last they had brought their terror into Europe.

The people of the village had seen the warning dust too late. But news of the calamity had traveled even faster than the Huns. The Gothic tribes who had settled in the district prepared to move on. They must go westward before they too fell victims to the massacre.

It was not the first time the Goths had moved. They were

indeed seldom in one place for long. Wooden cabins were sufficient for their shelter. Barley and wheat were what they lived on; and when the crops were harvested it was their custom to seek fresh fields. Theirs was a rough and simple life. They were used to fighting, and skilled in it, as many a Roman legion had found out to its cost. Sometimes, in fact, Gothic warriors from the north had been taken into the Roman army to make it stronger. But, courageous as they were, the Goths did not dare to stand before the ferocious Huns.

The Goths were the half-civilized tribes, the "barbarians," that so many Roman emperors had fought to keep out of the Empire. Already they had crossed the frontier here and there. Sometimes a barbarian tribe had been conquered, and brought into the Empire to till the soil. Sometimes a whole people had made a contract with the Empire, and become its "ally." They could not be shut out forever; for these were the new people of Europe, growing too numerous and strong for the weary forces of Rome to hold back.

They were coming anyway. With the Huns pressing them on, they had a reason for coming faster. The Goths made a bargain with the Roman emperor, to cross the Danube and then defend it against the Huns.

The gates were open now. The barbarians were inside. In larger numbers they began to pour in. They fought when they had to, and took land by force. Often, however, there was no need to fight. They simply settled down: uninvited guests who quickly made themselves at home. They began to marry with Roman citizens. Their leaders rose to high places in the service of the Empire.

Europe would never be the same again. The older Romans had called these tribes "barbarians." One day they would be Italians, Frenchmen, Germans. Meanwhile, a great darkness began to settle upon Europe. Where the barbarians came, schools disappeared. Theaters were closed. Towns became mere villages. People forgot how to speak good Latin.

In some places the change came about so gradually that nobody realized what had happened. But educated men remembered the glory of the Rome that once had been, and sighed for days of old. They wept to see the old Empire dying.

Far from Rome, in the town of Bethlehem where Christ was born, the great scholar Jerome was busy translating the Bible into Latin. But sometimes he thought of other things, and his thoughts were sad.

"A remnant of us survives," he wrote, "not by our merits, but by the mercy of God. Innumerable savage peoples have occupied the whole of Gaul. All that lies between the Alps and the Pyrenees, the Rhine and the Ocean, is devastated by the barbarians.... Time has dried our tears, and save for a few graybeards, the rest, born in captivity and siege, no longer regret the liberty of which the very memory is lost. But who could believe that Rome, on her own soil, fights no longer for glory, but for her existence?"

One calamity, men thought, would never happen. One stronghold of the ancient days would surely not be taken by the barbarian invaders. Rome itself, the Eternal City, the very center of the world, would never fall!

Yet in the year 410 it happened. Alaric, king of the Visigoths, marched upon Rome. Before he left, part of the city was in flames. Rome had been looted by a barbarian chief, and the Eternal City had fallen into the hands of uncivilized attackers.

In the days of Nero, Christians had been murdered because Rome was burned. The pagans who were left in Rome three hundred and fifty years after Nero could not take out their spite against the Church with anything but words. Helpless to do anything except complain, they once more charged that the Christians had brought down the anger of the gods upon the Roman Empire.

This time there was someone to answer for the Church. Across the Mediterranean Sea, in the North African town of Hippo, the great bishop Augustine heard of the calamity; and he heard also of the complaints of the pagans.

Augustine knew what pagan life was like, for he had tried it. Brought up by a Christian mother, he had lost his faith at school. Clever with words, he made his living by teaching others the art of how to speak and write. Loving the pleasures of life, he had had his fill of many sorts of sins, yet nothing had made him happy. There had been a restlessness in his soul, a longing for he knew not what.

But everything was changed for him one day as he sat in a garden, and heard a voice.

"Take up and read! Take up and read!" the voice was crying.

Was it, Augustine wondered, a child playing a game? Yet he knew of no game in which such words were used. It must be a command from God. Seizing the Letters of Saint Paul, he opened them at random, and his eyes fell upon what the apostle had written:

"Let us walk honestly, as in the day; not in rioting and drunkenness, not in chambering and wantonness, not in strife and envying: but put ye on the Lord Jesus Christ, and make not provision for the flesh, to fulfill the lusts thereof."

That had been over twenty years before the day that Alaric sacked Rome. Augustine was now a leader of the Church, and the greatest writer of his age. Upon himself he took the task of defending the Church against the charge that it had caused the ruin of the Empire. His answer was set down in a lengthy book which he called *The City of God*.

There have always, wrote Augustine, been calamities; and

they are a way by which God disciplines sinful men. It was not the faith of the Christians that brought this calamity upon Rome: it was the evil life of the pagans. In any case, said Augustine, there is a greater city than Rome. From the beginning of the world, he taught, there have been two cities. One was made up of those people who sought only earthly things. That kind of city could defend itself only by war, and sooner or later, like all earthly things, it would be destroyed. But there was another city, whose citizens were God's people, pilgrims on their way to heaven. That is the *City of God*; it will stand forever.

One thing was certain: the days of Rome's might were over. That earthly city had fallen. In the East, the emperor still ruled in power. In the West, Europe had fallen into the hands of the barbarians.

Where could men turn now—Romans or barbarians—except to the City of God? The Empire was being destroyed before their eyes, and all that was left was the Church.

The old Empire had had a ruler, as all empires must. The new empire, the Church, also had its ruler. He bore the title of "pope."

The pope was the bishop of Rome. From early times the Church at Rome had enjoyed great honor, because it was in the capital city of the Empire. As the Church was honored, so also was the bishop. It began to be said that the first bishop of Rome was actually the apostle Peter, although no one could prove that he was ever there. No one could speak highly enough of Peter. Men called him "the prince of the apostles," "the keeper of the kingdom of heaven," "the bearer of the keys," "the pillar." And of the bishops of Rome it was said that they had inherited Peter's power and glory. The pope also came to be called "the keeper of the kingdom of heaven."

There had been other cities that were great and honorable, and their churches and their bishops too were held in high respect. Jerusalem, Antioch, Alexandria, Ephesus, Corinth, and later Constantinople, all were powerful, and all were jealous of Rome. But those cities were all in the East, and western

Europe was now cut off from the East. Rome had no rivals any more. The power of the emperor's government was gone in Rome, but the Church was greater than ever. Among the ruins of the Empire, the pope stood up, stronger than he had ever been.

Even the barbarians admitted it. For the barbarians had also respected Rome, and could not imagine that it would ever fall. Even when it was besieged, looted, and sent up in flames and smoke, Rome was held in honor. And while rulers of the city might come and go, the ruler of the Church, the pope, stayed on.

Christians loved to tell of the time that Attila, the leader of the dreaded Huns, marched on Rome. It was the famous pope Leo the Great who led the delegation out to meet him. What was said at that meeting, no one knows; but Attila turned back and Rome was spared from his fury. The story was told that Attila saw a vision of the power of Saint Peter, and was afraid.

Whether or not Attila was afraid of the pope, others were. For he had, men said, the power to let souls into heaven or to keep them out. And that was a more terrible power than Caesar ever had. Rome was still great: because the pope was there.

It was not only in the presence of the pope that men felt that a strange and ghostly power had come among them. It was not scholars and bishops who made men think about the Church throughout the countryside. It was the monks.

The monks had first appeared in Egypt. Even before the persecutions ceased, men and women had gone out to the waste places, the lonely lands, into caves and deserts, there to live a special life far from the troubles of the world. It was not, however, to escape from difficulty that they fled to the open spaces. On the contrary, they believed that in the wastelands the demons lived, and it was against the demons that they longed to battle. Evil had its home out there, and on its own home ground they went to face it.

It had long been thought that there were two ways of Christian life: one, the ordinary way which a man might practice in his home and business; the other, the special kind of life which was for those who were willing to give up the world. To go without food and drink, and thus pass into that wonderful dream world which could be entered through fasting, was thought a way of coming near to God. To remain unmarried was considered a special virtue. In the days of safety that came when Constantine ended the persecution, growing numbers of people longed still to be heroic for Christ's sake. More and more they turned away from the Christianity that had become easy, and looked for the hard life, in which only the strong might succeed.

The monks who practiced this special way of life outdid one another in enduring hardships. Some ate nothing but grass, while others lived in trees. Still others refused to wash. Their reputation grew as fast as their numbers, and vast crowds of people came out from the cities to see them. One, Simeon Stylites, was so much troubled by crowds around the mouth of the cave where he lived, that he put up a pillar and made his home on the top of it for over thirty years. His food was sent up to him in a basket, and from time to time he preached to the multitudes below, converting thousands, we are told, to Christianity.

The monks lived all alone at first, until they were surrounded by admirers who were trying to imitate their way of living. Then the custom arose of building up a community of monks. Each one, or each group of two or three, lived in a separate cell. They met together for worship on Saturdays and Sundays. Apart from that, they lived to themselves, like hermits, each doing what he thought was best for the Christian life.

Finally they began to live together under one roof, in a monastery. The first organizer had been a soldier who knew how to discipline men. Each monk must work at some kind of toil, and what he made was sold to provide for the needs of all. A little later, monasteries were moved from the desert to the outskirts of the cities. In addition to physical labor, the duty of study was added to the requirements.

From the East, monasteries had spread to the West. It was Benedict, a man born in a noble family, who introduced a new system for the Western monks. He called it "a school for the service of God." The monastery was to be under the rule of an abbot, whose word was law. Four or five hours of the day were to be spent in worship. The rest of the day was for the most part to be used for manual labor, with time for rest and prayer and contemplation.

Thus came the monks to western Europe. Monasteries sprang up all over the land. Peasants at their toil could look up and see the roof of the nearby monastery, reminding them of the "holy men" who had given up the world to live for God alone. And the peasants knew that they themselves did not have to give up so much: they could be Christians too. But the monks were a special kind of Christians.

Two ways of living the Christian life had come to Europe—a higher and a lower way. There were men who had denied themselves their own property, their liberty, even their names. And the rest, who were not ready to make such sacrifices, were filled with awe. "We will give you food," they said, "if you will pray for us." For it was thought that any who gave up the pleasures of the world had the power to influence God in heaven.

CHAPTER 7

CONVERTING THE BARBARIANS

ON a hillside in northern Ireland, a boy of sixteen stood gazing into space. A herd of pigs were squealing around his feet, but young Patrick's thoughts were far away. Perhaps he thought of his comfortable home in Britain, from which pirates had kidnaped him only a few months before. There he had had Christian parents for companions; there he had known no want. Now he was all alone, in a land where Christians were few in number. Now he was a slave, living in misery, feeding swine.

Patrick's eyes closed, and he began to pray. His home was far away, but God was very near. It was good, after all, to be here on the wooded mountain. Here, in the lonely place, he could keep company with God.

Days lengthened into months, and months into years, and Patrick's love of God grew stronger. In one day he said a hundred prayers. He formed the habit of rising before daybreak, so that he might pray before his work began. The rain and the snow fell upon him, the frost bit into his flesh, but Patrick prayed; and even in the cold and the wet, God comforted him.

After six years of misery, in a dream there came a voice

which seemed to him divine. Obeying it, he fled to the seacoast, and there was a ship, ready to set sail! The captain was willing to take him aboard, if he would work his passage. Together with the crew, Patrick landed by accident in a remote part of France. With his companions, he stumbled through the desolate countryside for many days, and starvation nearly claimed the lives of all the party before help was found. Then Patrick set out to find his way home to Britain.

On the way he may have passed through Tours, in France, where the famous Martin had founded a monastery some fifty years before. Patrick would have listened spellbound to the stories of Martin—the former soldier who, in his army days, had once cut his military cloak in two to give half to a shivering beggar. Like Patrick, Martin had lived much in lonely forests. Even when he became bishop of Tours, he liked best to live quietly in his monastery, out of reach of the crowds. Patrick would have heard the story of how Martin converted a great number of pagans by defying a sacred tree. The pagans thought the tree divine, but Martin braved the anger of the gods. He agreed to stand where it would fall if it were cut down. To the amazement of the superstitious natives, it fell, not on Martin, but into the crowd. Most of all, Patrick would have loved to hear of how Martin prayed: for men said of him that never an hour passed when he was not engaged in prayer.

Home at last in England, Patrick had a dream; and in the dream there were voices again, voices from Ireland, crying, "We beseech thee, holy youth, to come and walk with us once more." To make ready for this journey, Patrick first went to Europe, and studied in great monasteries there. Before he sailed away from the continent, he was consecrated bishop of Ireland. Now he must return to the island where he had fed swine—this time to win the people to Jesus Christ.

In danger of death and robbery, Patrick traveled through Ireland, taking the gospel to perilous places where it had not been heard. Many were the tales that were told of him. It was said that he defied the pagans, and built an Easter fire beside a sacred spring. The high king of Ireland, who would at first have punished Patrick for his daring, became his friend, and Christianity came into the royal court. Through local chieftains Patrick reached the people. When he died in 461, almost the whole island had become Christian.

In the Roman Empire, Christianity had come first to the cities, and the bishops in the cities ruled the Church. In Ireland, the people lived, not in cities, but as tribes or clans upon the land. There were bishops to appoint the priests, but it was not the bishops who really ruled. The Church was led by the monasteries that Patrick founded. And these were not buildings such as Europe could boast of. They consisted of rude huts, made of boards and moss, to which was attached a church, usually called "the house of oak." Often they were built on islands, or around the coast. The Irish monks loved solitude. There they mingled with the songs of the old Irish poets the new strains of the Christian gospel. There they decorated their manuscripts of the Bible with strange and fantastic drawings. Remote from the continent of Europe, Ireland built up a kind of Church that was all its own. When Europe was plunged into darkness by the barbarians, the Irish monasteries were rich in poetry and art and learning.

If the Irish monks loved solitude, they also loved adventure. Three of them, it was said, "stole away from Ireland in a boat without oars, because they would live in a state of pilgrimage for the love of God—they cared not where." But others went away with a clearer purpose in their hearts. There was Columba of Donegal, who went with twelve companions to the island of Iona off the Scottish coast and became a missionary to the people of Scotland. Another Irishman, named Columbanus, sailed away not many years afterward, bound for France.

In France the Church was already strong. Clovis, the king of the Franks, had been converted in 496. Most of the other barbarian kings and chiefs who had overrun Europe were Arian Christians, who denied that Christ was equal with his Father. Clovis saw his chance to gain advantage by taking up the faith of the Roman Church. When he conquered rival nations, he forced this faith upon them, winning whole peoples to the Church, not by love but by the sword. The monasteries here and there throughout the country won many souls in a better way. Yet there were remote places where the Christian gospel did not reach.

To the wildest spot that he could find in France, Columbanus went with his companions. They were continually in danger of starvation. The land was like a jungle. The forest was filled with robbers. Going into caves to pray, the monks were often met by wild animals. Yet here their love of God and their venturesome spirit led them. Unarmed, frequently traveling alone, the missionaries from Ireland took the gospel into the lonely places of Europe.

Side by side with the peasant people, the Irish monks helped to clear the land. Lovers of nature themselves, they understood how it was that the peasants worshiped sacred trees and stones and wells. It was told of Columbanus that as he went through the woods the squirrels and the birds would come to him like puppies to their master. Monks like these could speak to the people of the countryside, when bishops and priests from distant cities would never have succeeded.

They kept the old holy places. The peasants could still worship where they used to come to honor their nature gods. The missionaries changed only the names of the gods. The peasants came to the old sacred shrines, and were told that they were honoring Christ, or the saints. Often the ignorant peasants did not know the difference. The new religion came and they accepted it, because so long as the old superstitions were kept, Christianity seemed like the religion they had always had. They became Christians in name without understanding what they believed.

Many Christians thought, however, that this was the only way to win barbarians to Christ. After the fierce Saxons had invaded Britain, and destroyed the Church that the Roman Empire planted there, missionaries had to come again to convert England to the gospel. To these missionaries it was no less a person than Pope Gregory the Great who gave the advice that idols should be destroyed, but not the temples of the idols. Keep the temples, he wrote, but use them for the worship of the one true God. The pagans are accustomed, he said, to sacrificing oxen to demons: then let them have their feasts, only see that they eat to the praise of Christ.

Only gradually, it seemed, would the barbarian peoples change from their old religions to the faith of the Christian Church. The trouble was, however, that they changed so gradually that many never knew what it was to be converted at all. To this very day, many ancient superstitions and customs of the countryside live on in Europe.

It was hard to know how best to fight the pagan worship. When Boniface, the great missionary from England, went into the heart of Germany, he told the people that the gods they worshiped were really devils. Before they could be received into the Christian Church, they must swear to abandon their old religion.

"Dost thou forsake the devil?" the missionary would ask.

The new Christian would respond, "I forsake the devil."

"And all the devil's wage?"

"And I forsake all the devil's wage."

"And all the devil's works?"

"And I forsake all the devil's works and words, Thunor and Woden and Saxnot, and all the fiends that are their company."

Then, and only then, could the convert confess his faith in the Father, Son, and Holy Spirit.

It was at the peril of his life that any missionary went among these people. Boniface himself became a bishop, and head of all the Church in Germany. Yet in the end he was murdered by a band of pagans. Seeing no opportunity for escape, and no chance of winning over the murderers, Boniface spoke while there still was time to the men who must die with him that day:

"Be strong in the Lord, and suffer willingly that which he permits.... Brothers, be of a brave mind, and fear not those that kill the body, but cannot kill the soul that has an endless life. Rejoice in the Lord, and fix on him the anchor of your hope."

Having thus spoken, Boniface paid the price of his great mission. And by such sacrifices the gospel was carried to the far frontiers of Europe.

There were, however, those who sought an easier way to win the heathen for the Church. When a chief or a king could be converted, he might compel his subjects to accept baptism too. It was his decision, and not theirs. Thus did many become members of the Church, not because they believed in it or even understood it, but only because they were told to do so. The numbers of Church members grew, but the number who wanted to be Christians was not so large. Even where the Church seemed strong, it was often really weak. It was built on the power of kings and governments, not on the faith of the common people.

Sometimes the gospel of love was spread by cruel deeds. Charlemagne, king of the Franks, went among the Saxons in the forests and swamps of northern Germany, determined to make Christians of these stubborn people. He did it by slaughter and by treachery. In one day he massacred forty-five hundred warriors who had surrendered. Then he retired to winter quarters, to celebrate Christmas and wait for Easter. He issued laws that anyone who entered a church and robbed it should be put to death. Anyone who despised the holy season of Lent by eating meat should likewise die; and the death penalty was decreed for any who should hide to escape from baptism.

For twenty-five years he kept the warfare up. He would allow no clergymen to accompany his armies, for fear they would see how his victories were won. But after every conquest he sent for priests; and they were kept busy baptizing the people who survived the slaughter.

In the end the Saxons were almost all baptized. But they had not yet known what Christian teaching meant, and beneath the surface they were pagan still. Worse than that, there was bitterness in the hearts of the victims. For they had become Christian only to save their lives.

Thus by monks and monarchs, by saints and by the sword, step by step the whole of northern Europe was brought under the dominion of the Church.

CHAPTER 8

THE ROUGH CENTURIES

By the panting war-horses,
Striking fire from their hoofs,
Charging at dawn,
Under a cloud of dust
Piercing the enemy host—
Truly man is ungrateful toward his Lord,
And he himself is witness of his ingratitude;
For truly his heart is set on worldly gain.
Does he not know that, when the graves are opened,
All in the breasts of men shall be as daylight?

A GROUP of admirers listened while the fierce poetry poured from the lips of Mohammed, a former camel driver of Arabia. The words must not be forgotten. They must be written in the Koran, the sacred book of Mohammed's sayings.

But there were enemies to fight, and they would not be conquered by words alone. At dawn the men would ride forth: lean, black-eyed men, riding the swift and hardy horses of the desert. And if they should die, they would not go to the hell

63

that they had been taught to fear. For they were Moslems; their religion was Islam, "submission to God." Fighting for Allah, the God in whose name Mohammed spoke, they knew that death would but bring them into that paradise of which their prophet told them. They would come to a place of coolness, where clear streams flowed. There they would eat the fruit that grew on trees without thorns, or lie on easy couches and quench their thirst with the heavenly drink of which a man might take his fill without falling into drunkenness. Wives would be there for them: beautiful maidens whose eyes glistened like black pearls.

Yet they expected not death but victory. The angels of Allah would fight with them. The war horses of the Moslems would pierce the enemy host.

The cry went up: "There is no God but Allah, and Mohammed is his prophet!"

Mohammed had been poor in boyhood, but success in trade had made him rich. Trade had brought him not only wealth, but knowledge as well. Traveling with his caravans, he learned to know his own Arab people, and also Jews and Christians, with whom his business dealings brought him into touch. The Arabs of the inland desert had lived for centuries by keeping sheep. Back and forth across the wilderness they roved, always on the move, looking for pastures for their flocks. For religion they worshiped the gods and goddesses of the places where they halted, holding in reverence many rocks and trees and wells, fearing the wild spirits that roamed the desert. Even in the town of Mecca, Mohammed's home, religion was not much better. At the square temple called the Kaaba the idols of the town were kept; and the Kaaba was especially holy because it contained a great black stone, said to have fallen from heaven. Even from distant places, hosts of pilgrims every year made their way to Mecca to visit this sacred shrine.

How much better, Mohammed thought, was the religion of Jews and Christians! The conviction came to him that there is only one God, Allah, framer of all creation, who demands that men live rightly in this world. At the judgment day, Allah will punish the wicked and reward the good. This God, Mohammed claimed, is the same God that Jews and Christians worship. He has had many prophets: Moses, Abraham, Noah, and Jesus were his spokesmen. But the Christians, Mohammed thought, were wrong in believing in the Trinity: for it seemed to him that Father, Son, and Holy Spirit were three gods, not one.

When he was over forty years of age, Mohammed had a vision. The angel Gabriel appeared to him, and delivered the message that convinced the wealthy Arab that he was chosen to be the last and greatest of the prophets. His teachings at first made him many enemies, but supporters joined him and his fame began to spread. When he died in 632, he controlled the town of Mecca. The idols of the shrine were cast out, but the great black stone remained. And when the worshipers of Allah prayed, five times a day, it was toward Mecca that they turned their faces.

After Mohammed's death, the new religion of Islam began to gain successes greater than when the founder was alive. It swept through Arabia, and from there into neighboring lands. Poor for so long, the Arabs were hungry for conquest to bring them wealth. The pride of their race drove them on; and in their new faith all the Arab tribes were at last united. They poured into Persia, into Syria, into Egypt.

Victories were won easily. To many people in the invaded lands, Islam seemed the best religion they had ever known. It was easy to understand; and it taught a pure and simple life, which would surely be rewarded at the last day. Christian teaching was far more difficult to grasp. Besides, it paid to become Moslems. For conquered peoples who kept their own religion had to pay tribute to their victors, and by joining Islam they could escape this burden. Sometimes enthusiastic Moslems slaughtered their opponents, or forced them to accept the faith under the threat of death. The leaders, however, did not approve of needless massacre, for they preferred to have the vanquished live and pay taxes.

The Christian empire in the East, with its capital at

Constantinople, barely saved itself from destruction. The Arab power swept on, winning Asia as far east as India. Westward across Africa it pushed, wiping out the Christian Church—the Church of Africa, so strong in the days of Augustine. Not content with that, it invaded Spain. One hundred years after the death of Mohammed, Islam had become the Church's most dangerous rival. Countless souls had been won to the new faith, never in this world to return to Christ.

In 732, the Moslems were pressing northward. They raided the land where France now lies, then inhabited by the Franks, a German people. But here at last they were thrown back. A Frankish ruler defeated the armies of Islam near Poitiers, in one of the important battles of the world. The Franks were saved, and Europe was filled with rejoicing. The hero of the hour earned the name of Charles Martel—"Charles the Hammer." The hammer blow of his army halted the Moslems, and they advanced no farther.

Pope Leo III knew that he was unpopular. His foes declared that he had been guilty of immoral conduct. A good many people probably resented the fact that the pope was acting more like a king than like a pastor of Christ's Church.

But Leo did not suspect to what lengths his enemies were planning to go. As he set out upon a procession, one day in the year 799, a band of ruffians suddenly leaped from hiding. The long train of attendants accompanying the pope quickly fled from the scene. His assailants lifted him from his horse, and began to beat him with clubs. Some of them tried to pull out his eyes. Aided by some friends, Leo escaped down a wall by a rope, and managed—injured and half blind though he was—to get to St. Peter's Church. There he was met by a French duke, who escorted him safely home.

It was not the first time a pope had had to get help from the Franks. After all, it was a Frankish leader who had thrown back the Moslems. When the savage nation of Lombards had threatened to overrun Italy, a Frankish king had defeated them, and given to the pope then reigning a little country all his own.

True, the pope still paid allegiance to the emperor who ruled the luxurious court of Constantinople; and for his own part he claimed to be supreme over the Church in the East just as in the West. But East and West were drifting far apart. In the East, the Church was safe under the protection of the emperor's throne. Bishops lived in ease, but they paid a price for safety: the emperor who protected them also ruled them, and they could not call their souls their own.

In the rough struggles of western Europe, the pope must fend for himself. He must have protection; and it would not come from distant Constantinople. It would have to come from France. Leo made up his mind to visit the Frankish king.

The king was at this time Charles—the grandson of Charles Martel, and the same monarch who converted the Saxons to Christianity by bloody war. At home he was a more pleasant person than when he marched with his troops. Though he could not write, he could read. His delight was to browse through books of history and astronomy; his favorite book of all was Augustine's *City of God*. He loved the society of scholars, among whom he dropped all differences of rank and went simply by the name of David. Under his encouragement, scholars made the Latin language pure again, bringing back correct spelling and good writing after the ignorance spread by the barbarian invasions. Schools were set up throughout the kingdom; clergymen were urged to educate themselves. To the Church, Charles gave lavish gifts.

At the head of the palace school was Alcuin, the greatest scholar of his time, who lived on the most intimate terms with Charles. Alcuin prepared the king for the pope's visit by a letter. There had been up until now, Alcuin said, three persons greater than all others in the world. One was his supreme holiness the pope. The second had been the emperor at Constantinople, but now the emperor was weak. The third, Alcuin continued, "is the royal dignity in which the decree of our Lord Jesus Christ has placed you as ruler of the Christian people, more excellent in power than the other aforesaid dignities, more illustrious in wisdom, more sublime in the dignity of your kingdom. Lo! now on you alone the salvation of the Churches of Christ falls and rests. You are the avenger of crimes, the guide of wanderers, the comforter of mourners, the exalter of the good."

It was in 799 that the pope journeyed to see Charles; and in 800 the king returned the visit. His business in Rome was to clear up the accusations of wickedness with which the pope was charged, and to deal with the enemies who had attacked Leo in the street. The pope swore to his innocence, and the conspirators were banished from Italy.

On Christmas Day, King Charles went to St. Peter's Church for worship. Out of courtesy to Leo, he had laid aside his picturesque Frankish costume—his tunic with the silver border, his vest of otterskin and sable, his blue cloak—and put on Roman clothes. As he knelt before the altar, the pope approached him. He placed on Charles's head a golden crown, and over his Roman tunic he threw the purple mantle of empire.

The crowd cried out: "To Charles, most pious and august, crowned by God, the great and peace-bringing emperor, be life and victory." Then the multitude burst into a hymn of praise.

Thus a new empire in the West was born. It was destined to be known as the Holy Roman Empire, and to last, in name at least, for a thousand years. Henceforth its first ruler would be called Charlemagne—"Charles the Great."

Yet Charlemagne was not entirely pleased by what had happened. It was not that he objected to the honor. But he probably would have preferred to crown himself. If it was the head of the Church who appointed rulers, who was going to be supreme in the empire—the emperor or the pope?

Uneasy about the way he had won the crown, Charlemagne confided to a friend: "Would I had never entered St. Peter's on Christmas Day!"

Charlemagne was strong; yet even he could not unite the many nations that lived within his empire. When he was gone, and weaker men sat upon the throne, greater darkness than before settled down on Europe. The age of feudalism had arrived.

It was no privilege to be free in those harsh days. What everyone wanted was protection; and all save the greatest were willing to sell their liberty to get it. Barons offered their services to kings; and smaller men offered themselves to barons. For the privilege of cultivating a little patch of land, a man would agree to fight in the private army of the nearest lord. In this way he not only got a living from the soil, but helped to protect his home from the private army of some other lord.

All across western Europe, one would see small plots of land surrounding villages. Cities and towns were rare, and there were few who earned their livelihood by making or selling goods. The people lived upon the soil. The common people made their homes in huts of stone or clay, with thatched roofs. Across these little dwellings fell the shadow of the lord's manor house, built of hewn logs, and made more imposing by a tower of stone.

When there were battles to fight, the humble peasants followed up on foot the charges made by knights on horseback. The romance of war appealed to the highborn: their ambition was to do valiant deeds on the field of battle. A youth of noble family had to choose whether he would enter the Church or become a knight: there was no other career open to him. If he chose the Church, he might rise to become a bishop; and as a bishop he might have lands and armies at his service, for the Church too had become a feudal lord like the barons of the time. A humbler work of religion was to enter a monastery, where the monks kept alive what little knowledge there was in those dark centuries, poring over the few and precious manuscripts which were almost worn through with much reading.

The more adventurous youths, however, aspired to knighthood. They could not inherit it: they had to earn it. As boys they were taught to play with wooden weapons, then to break in horses, and to join the hunt. When at last a young man was considered worthy to bear the title of knight, he dressed in white clothes and took Holy Communion. Then his armor was put on him, and he knelt and made his vows. Finally he would feel the blow on the back of his neck, delivered by the flat of a sword, and hear the words, "In the name of God, I make thee knight." Now he could take the sword himself, and with it win honor and protect the weak.

The adventure-loving lords and knights glorified the warfare in which they were continually engaged. Tales of valor were told and retold. Later a code of honor, which included especially the protection of women, would make the calling of the warrior seem almost holy. But the heads of the Church saw the constant strife in a different light. They saw that farms were being overrun and ruined, that men mixed their so-called honor with cruelty, that precious lives were daily being lost in the private feuds and wars that never ceased. Vainly the Church tried to check the evil with what was called the Truce of God: an order that there should be no fighting between Thursday evening and Monday morning, nor at certain holy seasons of the year. Still the warfare raged throughout the countryside of Europe.

It was the pope Urban II who thought of a better plan. If Christian men must fight, let them not fight each other, but go to war against the Moslems. There were other advantages in the plan as well. If the Church in western Europe could go to the rescue of the Church in the East, perhaps East and West could be united once again. Moreover, the pope would be the hero of the story, for it was his idea, and he meant to organize it under his own leadership.

In the year 1095, Pope Urban crossed to France, without saying anything to the emperor about his plans. At Clermont he made a speech to a great gathering which had come to hear him. He told his audience that he had had word of atrocities done by the Moslems in the Holy Land. They had captured the Holy Sepulcher, the tomb of Christ. They were torturing Christians and desecrating churches. Jerusalem cried out for aid.

A Frenchman at home among his people, speaking their own language, Urban knew how to work upon the feelings of his hearers. Excitement was rising to fever pitch.

"On whom," he demanded, "will fall the task of vengeance if not upon you who have already won glory in combat? Come forward to the defense of Christ!"

A mighty shout interrupted him: "God wills it!"

"Set forth, then," Urban continued, "upon the road to the Holy Sepulcher. Go forth, fearing nothing. I see before you, leading you to war, the standard-bearer who is invisible—the Lord Christ!"

The movement was quickly organized. Mounted heralds went from place to place, wearing red crosses, to make known the pope's call to arms. Protection was guaranteed those who answered the summons. Their families would be safe; their property would be awaiting them on their return. Those who perished might be sure of entrance into heaven.

Thousands responded to the call. The towns of Italy, hoping to increase their trade in the East, were ready to give financial help. In 1096 a great host of men, each wearing a cross sewn to his clothes, set out upon the First Crusade. By the summer of 1099, Jerusalem fell to the Crusaders. Countless Moslems were slaughtered, and the leader of the conquering forces was elected Defender of the Holy Sepulcher.

The glad news was brought home, and the mighty deeds of the victors became the talk of Europe. There was one, however, who did not live to hear the story. Pope Urban died in the same month that Jerusalem fell.

Had he learned the news, he would have died rejoicing. No one could know then that the triumph was less than it seemed. No one could foresee that Crusade after Crusade would set forth in the two centuries ahead, and that in the long run the Moslems would recapture Jerusalem. No one could tell how many lives would be thrown away in the far-off places of the Holy Land. No one could realize that Islam, having won so much of the world by the sword, was too strong to be vanquished in the same way. Nor could anyone see as yet that the Church of the East and the Church of the West were doomed to remain apart.

Yet Urban would have been glad to know about the victory. He could have said, "The pope has triumphed!" And in that he would have been right. For popes and emperors were going to struggle for the highest place in the Holy Roman Empire. The men who sat on Saint Peter's throne after Urban could be thankful for the glory that the pope had brought himself, without an emperor's help. And the emperors to come, hating the power of the pope, like Charlemagne might curse that Christmas Day when the king of the Franks entered St. Peter's Church.

CHAPTER 9

MEN OF POWER

TEN years before the Crusades began, a pope named Gregory VII lay dying at Salerno on the southwest coast of Italy. Out to sea, many centuries earlier, the ship must have passed bearing Paul to Rome as a prisoner. Gregory himself was little better than a prisoner now. Certainly he dared not return to Rome, even if he had the strength. But if his mind was on any of the apostles, it was most likely Peter of whom he was thinking. For he declared that when he spoke as pope, he was speaking with no less than the voice of Saint Peter, prince of the apostles.

Gregory was a small man, and his birth had been humble. Hildebrand was his name before he rose to occupy Saint Peter's throne. But in the Church even a peasant could become great: there was no limit to the opportunities that the Church offered. As pope, Gregory had been the greatest man of his time.

He had lived for his ideals, and he had tolerated nothing that in his eyes weakened or shamed the Church. Thinking back over his career, it seemed to him that he had always been right. Surely he ought not to be dying in this fashion! He did not doubt that he was right in insisting that priests of the Roman Church should follow the ancient custom of not marrying. Should priests live like other men?

He was equally sure that he was right in trying to keep kings from meddling in Church affairs. When Gregory became pope, kings were selling the high positions in the Church to those who were willing to pay for them. Kings were treating bishops like the feudal lords or barons of their realms. They were even taking it upon themselves to conduct the solemn ceremonies by which a bishop was installed in his post, giving the new bishop the ring and staff which were the symbols of his authority.

Gregory had forbidden all this. The Church, he said, must be ruled from Rome. There was a time when kings had had to step to his command. He had excommunicated King Henry IV of Germany—suspended him from the Church—and told Henry's subjects that they were free to choose another king. Henry had had to come crawling to him then. The dying pope remembered with satisfaction how he kept the king waiting barefoot in the snow for three days, outside the castle at Canossa, before he would even let him in.

But that was back in 1077. Unfortunately for the pope, King Henry lived to get his revenge. The king brought an army to Rome and captured the city. He appointed another pope, who crowned Henry as head of the Holy Roman Empire. In the fighting that followed, Gregory had to flee. He could hardly venture to go back—for a great part of Rome was lying in ruins; and men, women, and children had been led away like cattle into slavery by the brutal allies that Gregory had unwisely summoned to his aid.

Now death was stealing upon him in the warm weather of early summer. Fair was the countryside without, but gloomy were Gregory's thoughts within. It was bitter to have failed. Gregory cried out, "I have loved righteousness and hated iniquity; therefore I die in exile"; and with those words he died.

But the ideal for which he lived did not die with him. Gregory had not really failed. The Crusades brought glory to the Church, when armies marched eastward, not at the command of king or emperor but at the summons of a pope. Kings came and went, and fought with one another to hold their kingdoms. Popes could look down on half a continent, and call all Christian men their subjects. Wise popes, believing they had inherited divine power from Saint Peter, knew how to hold their own against ambitious kings who had to struggle for their crowns. One time a pope refused to crown an emperor until the proud ruler agreed to hold the stirrup to help the pope dismount from his horse.

A century passed by, and a young pope named Innocent III was raised to Saint Peter's throne. Now at last the time had come to seize the kind of power that Gregory VII had longed for. Innocent was the man to see an opportunity, and he was quick to take advantage of an opponent. Had he been born of royal blood, he would have made a brilliant emperor himself; but no emperor had more power than he. Whether in business, in politics, in government, or in diplomacy, his genius was equal to any task. It was not enough for him to rule the Church. He must also rule the nations. It was as though, having been taken into a high mountain and shown all the kingdoms of the world, he had decided to govern them all. From his exalted place in Rome he busied himself continually in the affairs of nations. He played off kings against kings in the great game of getting power for the pope. If disputes arose among rulers, they were often settled at his footstool. In Italy he himself reigned as a monarch.

All this, said Innocent, was as it ought to be. For the pope, he taught, is Christ's vicar—his deputy—on earth. Just as the spirit rules over the body, so the Church rules the world.

The power of the Church, Innocent said, is like the sun; the power of human rulers is like the moon, which gets its light only as a pale reflection from the sun. "Kings," he wrote, "rule over their kingdoms, but Peter rules over the whole earth. The Lord Jesus Christ has set up one ruler over all things; and as all things in heaven, earth, and hell bow the knee to Christ, so should all obey Christ's vicar, that there be one flock and one shepherd."

Pope Innocent III gazed thoughtfully at his visitor, and frowned a little. He was not angry so much as puzzled. Had this person been a king, a baron, or a bishop, Innocent would have known how to deal with him. But the man had a kind of power to which the pope was not accustomed.

The visitor stood in his bare feet. He had nothing he could call his own except the clothes he wore: and these were worn and ragged garments that someone else had thrown away. His name was Francis; but he liked best to be known as "the little poor one."

He had not always been so poor. He had, in fact, been a gay young blade: a spoiled child, with all the money he wanted to squander on his own pleasures. He was still gay enough. Men called him "God's minstrel"; and sometimes he was seen drawing a stick across his arm, as though playing a violin, while he sang hymns. "An odd character," thought Innocent. The pope could understand why the good people of Assisi, where Francis had been brought up, had thought the young man mad. Francis' own father, a rich and perfectly respectable cloth merchant, had come to the same conclusion, and had disowned his son. It was bad enough that Francis should embrace lepers and kiss their filthy sores, but what alarmed the old merchant most was the amount of money his son was giving away.

The father's patience had come to an end, when Francis, because of a voice he claimed to have heard, took a load of cloth from the shop and gave the price he got for it to repair a broken-down church. The merchant took the young man to the bishop's court, to denounce him as a false and unworthy son. Francis was only too willing to give up every claim to his family wealth. He stripped off his clothes, and instantly the bishop flung his own robe around the young man's body. Then Francis addressed his father:

"Until now I have called you my father on earth. But from now on I can confidently say, 'Our Father, which art in heaven,' on whom I have set all my trust and hope!"

The bishop was moved with pity, and had a peasant's cloak brought to Francis. This he accepted, and, having chalked a cross on the tattered garment, "God's minstrel" went out to become a messenger of God's love.

Soon he had his disciples. They called themselves the Friars Minor—"the lesser brothers." An abandoned travelers' shelter, near a leper hospital, was their first headquarters; and this was so small that Francis had to chalk the name of each friar over the place where he was to sleep. The only rule that the friars had to follow was the one Jesus had given to the twelve disciples, just as it stood in Saint Matthew's Gospel:

> And as ye go, preach, saying, The kingdom of heaven is at hand. Heal the sick, cleanse the lepers, raise the dead, cast out devils: freely ye have received, freely give. Provide neither gold, nor silver, nor brass in your purses; nor scrip for your journey, neither two coats, neither shoes, nor yet staves: for the workman is worthy of his meat.

Now Francis had come to Innocent, to get the pope's approval for his band of poor friars. The pope hardly knew what to say. Views like these might be dangerous. Indeed, there had been a French merchant named Peter Waldo, who not many years before had begun to teach similar ideas. He had organized a group of Poor Men, who devoted themselves to Christian work among the people and believed none of the teachings of the Church except what they could find for themselves in the New Testament. This could not be tolerated. It was for priests and bishops to decide what the Church believed. Francis might be another man of the same type.

The pope was half inclined to say no to the request of "the little poor ones." Francis might be sincere, but his rule of absolute poverty did not seem very practical in this hard world. Could men really live and obey such a rule? But one of the pope's advisers spoke up and said,

"If we say that it is impossible to follow what is taught in the gospel, we shall blaspheme against Christ, who is the author of the gospel."

Innocent saw that he would have to be careful. Francis certainly appeared to have the gospel on his side. The pope announced that he would give his decision another day.

That night Innocent had a dream. As he lay in his bed, he saw a vision of a great church tottering and about to fall. Then a poor man, barefoot and dressed in peasant clothes, put his shoulder under the doomed cathedral and propped it upon his back.

The next day, when the pope and the little friar were again face to face, Francis told a story. There was once, he said, a rich king who married a poor woman. Though the mother was poor, the sons always had enough to eat.

"Now," asked Francis, "is it to be feared that the sons and heirs of the everlasting King will perish of hunger, however poor they be?"

The pope was convinced. He gave his approval to the new order of friars, and commissioned them to go out, even though they were not priests, and preach repentance.

It was a wise decision. The power of love in the hearts of "the little poor folk" was saved for the Church, and they were not driven away. Walking barefoot through the land, the friars won the devotion of thousands. They were of more value than the monks. When the monks gave up the world, they retired to monasteries. The friars stayed in the world, to preach to men. Into the new towns, beginning to grow rich with trade, they went as humble ministers of Christ, while the monks, remote in their great landed estates, did not touch the life of the common people any more.

As for Francis himself, he became known as the very "mirror of perfection." Many were the stories told of him, and nothing was thought too wonderful to be believed. All living things were to Francis his brothers and his sisters. It was repeated widely that he melted the heart of a ferocious wolf, and made him promise to do no more harm to man or beast. The story went abroad that he preached to his sisters, the birds, and that they opened their beaks and bowed to the ground in reverence. He could not bear to put out a flame, because he loved it so. And when his eyes were blinded with so much weeping for his sins, and the physician ordered a hot iron to be drawn across the face of the saint, Francis then spoke thus: "My brother fire, noble and useful among all other creatures, be kindly in this hour."

Before he died, it was said that he received on his hands and feet the marks of the nailprints of Jesus' cross. And when death was very near, he added a verse to a song he had composed. In his song, he had bidden all God's creatures sing their Maker's praise—brother sun, "beautiful and radiant with great splendor," sister moon and the stars, "clear and precious and comely," brother wind and sister water, brother fire, and sister mother earth. But in death's hour he called upon another friend in the verse he added: "Be thou praised, my Lord, of our sister death."

Innocent III was never wiser than when he blessed the poor friars of Francis. All the pope's influence and wealth could never have purchased spiritual power like that. Two years after his death, Francis received an honor that was never conferred upon the magnificent pope who first permitted him to preach. He was declared one of the saints of the Church: he would be called Saint Francis.

Innocent was wise again when he gave permission to a man named Dominic to found another company of traveling preachers. Dominic's plan was to take his men through southern France, and by preaching convert the many thousands of people there who had fallen away from the Roman Church and taken up a strange religion known as Albigensianism. Like Francis, Dominic and his men went barefoot, begging their living when necessary, having no possessions save the buildings in which they slept together. They marked themselves as Dominicans by a white woolen garment, covered by a black cloak. They became known as the Friars Preachers, or Black Friars, while the followers of Francis were the Gray Friars. Soon the costumes of both these orders were familiar throughout Europe, as their ranks grew to number tens of thousands.

Beginning as preachers, the Dominicans became great in

learning. It was a day of opportunity for scholars. After the long night of the Dark Ages, when what little learning men possessed was kept alive mainly in monastery cells, Europe had grown hungry for knowledge. Universities were springing up in Italy, France, England, Spain, Germany. Scholars had discovered once again the writings of the Greek thinkers who lived before the time of Christ. From the Moslem Arabs they learned philosophy, science, arithmetic, and algebra. A young man who wished to be a student was wise to become a friar; although he could own nothing for himself, he would be able to live in a comfortable building, and be provided with food and drink, light and heat, and a library in which to feast his mind.

About the time of Francis' death, and not many years after Dominic had died, a man who was to be known as Thomas Aquinas was born. He was of noble birth, and the cousin of a king. But he was not interested in royal honors, or the power and wealth that a lord could have. Even as a child of five, there was one question that he was forever asking his teachers: "What is God?" Seeing that he was so interested in religion, his family would have made him the head of a monastery, as befitted his high station in society. But as Thomas grew to manhood, he chose instead the white and black costume of the Dominican friars. To the furious disappointment of his family, he left home to become a barefoot preacher.

He was a fat, slow-moving man, and he got the nickname of "the great dumb ox of Sicily." But "the dumb ox" turned out to have the greatest mind of his age. He became a university teacher. He gathered together all the wisdom of the Greeks and Arabs, all the learning and all the doctrine of the Church as it had passed down through the centuries. What he wrote in his books is to this day the teaching of the Roman Catholic Church. Instead of "the dumb ox," Thomas Aquinas came to be called by another name: "the angelic doctor."

Great indeed was Innocent III. He was the master of kings and kingdoms. He blessed the poor Franciscans with their gospel rule of poverty and love. He gave his blessing also to the Dominicans, who soon could claim the greatest scholar of the Roman Church. But Innocent was not satisfied to make the Church great through politics, or preaching, or learning, or love. He did not trust in these alone. He was determined to defend the Christian faith by brute force as well.

To disagree with the teachings of the Church was called heresy: and heresy had long been against the law. From the time of the emperor Constantine, men had occasionally been punished for opposing the doctrines held by the rulers of the Church. Now, however, Innocent declared that heresy was the worst of crimes—worse than treason against a king: for it was treason against God Almighty. The punishment ought therefore to be more severe than for any other crime.

Ordinary ways of trial and punishment would not work, for there were too many heretics. The south of France was full of Albigensians, and against them Innocent called for a crusade. Those who took part in this holy war would gain pleasant lands and orchards if they lived, and reward in heaven if they died. Men who loved cruelty and bloodshed were glad of a chance to kill with the pope's blessing on them. At one castle the defeated heretics had their eyes torn out and their noses cut off. Elsewhere a woman was thrown into a well and buried under a crushing weight of stones. How many were burned to death no one knows. Even the pope was shocked, but when the massacre had begun, he could not halt it.

Horrible as the slaughter was, it did not wipe out the Albigensians. After the death of Innocent, another pope gave permission to the Dominican friars to search out and try all suspected heretics in the south of France. Trials were held in secret. The victim could be tortured to make him confess his error and come back to the Church. Even then he might be put to death. Men's souls, it was thought, might be saved by the suffering of their bodies. The system soon spread under the dread name of the Inquisition. By the time the century was over, in most nations a heretic could be punished—if lighter punishment did not seem sufficient—by burning at the stake.

Long centuries before, in the days of the Roman Empire, torture had been permitted. The Christians were the victims then, for the pagans were in power and the Church was small. Now the Church was in power, and the Church brought back the worst evils of the pagan empire. Christians had become cruel for the sake of Christ.

Through the work of preachers, many souls were won. Words and deeds of love converted many, and learning made them wise. But if these things failed, the Church had other weapons with which to spread the gospel—war, bloodshed, terror, imprisonment, racks to stretch men's bodies, thumbscrews to crush their fingers, fire to consume their flesh. Great was the Church, and pitiless to any who dared defy it. In piercing screams of agony, many a wretched soul had to admit that the Church had become strong indeed.

CHAPTER 10

THE CHURCH DECAYS

THE great crowd surged forward through the Roman street. Everyone was fighting for space in which to breathe, but nobody wanted to withdraw from the throng. Safely to one side, a little group of pilgrims watched the multitude struggling toward its goal.

"Have you seen it yet?" one of the men asked his neighbor.

"No," replied the other, "I got to Rome only this morning. I wouldn't want to go into that crowd today!"

"Well, it was no better yesterday, and it will be the same tomorrow. The day I went to see it, a man was crushed to death near this very place."

"Where are they all going?" a boy asked.

"They are going to see Saint Veronica's towel," was the answer.

"But who was Saint Veronica?"

"They say she was one of the women of Jerusalem who followed Jesus when he was taken out to be crucified. She gave him a towel to wipe the sweat from his face, and the marks are still on that towel!"

"The Savior's face!" The lad was dumfounded. He had

83

known that in Rome he would view the tomb of Saint Peter; but he had not counted on seeing any object so sacred as a handkerchief that had touched the face of Christ. In his heart a wild hope sprang up afresh. Perhaps if he could come close enough to the towel, the withered arm that hung useless at his side would at last be healed.

He had touched the bones of a saint long dead, and that had not helped. Another time he had kissed a tattered bit of cloth that a martyr once had worn, and still he was not healed. Why were so many miracles done for others, and not for him? If only his father were rich! Then he might buy one of the pieces of Jesus' clothing that Crusaders had brought back from the Holy Land. He had prayed and prayed to the Virgin Mary; and he wondered if he might not someday go to her house, which angels had carried all the way from Palestine to Italy, and there receive the answer to his prayers. But here, in Rome, was Saint Veronica's towel—and that might heal him.

With his good hand he pulled at his father's sleeve.

"Look—there is a place where we can get into the crowd. Let's go today!"

The father hesitated. He knew what the boy was thinking; and he was not sure that just seeing the towel would bring a miracle. That had not been the purpose of this journey to Rome. They had come because, in this year 1300, the pope had proclaimed a jubilee to celebrate the beginning of a new century. All who came to St. Peter's Church and sincerely confessed their sins would be forgiven.

But a cloth that had wiped Jesus' face was something no one should fail to see. In his heart the father was almost as eager as the boy—as eager as that vast, milling crowd who were ready to risk life and limb for a glimpse of the holy relic.

Father and son melted into the throng, and soon were lost from sight—two trusting souls among the countless thousands who believed everything that the Church told them.

From an upper window another man watched the crowds below with satisfaction. It was the old pope, Boniface VIII.

His jubilee was proving a great success. He was informed that thirty thousand people were daily streaming in and out of Rome. At the altar in St. Peter's Church two men were on duty day and night, gathering in with rakes the coins brought by the faithful pilgrims as their offering. The money was important, but what mattered even more to Boniface was the proof that such vast numbers of people still were loyal to the Church. This, he thought, would be a good century for popes.

He was glad of this encouragement, for he had been having trouble with rebellious kings. Neither the king of England nor the king of France had been so obedient to the pope as he ought to be. But seeing these immense crowds before St. Peter's, could even a king doubt the power of the pope?

Boniface had no doubts. He would be as great as Innocent III—no, even greater! Already he had forbidden kings to tax the Church without the pope's permission. Now he was ready to go farther. A Scripture text came into his mind. It was from Saint Luke, in the story of Jesus' last night with his disciples: "And they said, Lord, behold, here are two swords. And he said unto them, It is enough."

Boniface prepared to write his next message to the world. The two swords spoken of in the Gospel, he would say, stood for spiritual power and worldly power: and both belonged to the Church. When kings used force, when they sent out armies or police, it must be for the sake of the Church and on orders from the priest. Moreover, Boniface insisted, obedience to the pope was necessary for the salvation of every human creature.

Thus did Boniface dream of a stronger empire than any pope had ruled before. But the dream never came true. The foolish old man did not know how times were changing. Once kings had taken orders from the Church because they had to. Things were different now. Kings were stronger, and more sure of their crowns. Kings were growing independent. King Philip the Fair of France thought that the pope had gone too far; and the king was not afraid.

Only three years after the happy jubilee of 1300, Philip accused Pope Boniface of every crime that he could think of, and then sent a party of ruffians to Italy to arrest him. Whether the pope was guilty of any crime or not did not particularly matter to the king. Boniface was treated to rough words and a few blows, and thrown into a dungeon. Shortly afterward he was released. His body was not badly hurt, but his pride was wounded more than he could bear. Within a month he was on his deathbed. He refused to take food, and he beat his head against the wall. Out of his mind, he imagined that everyone who came near him was trying to put him into prison. "He reigned like a lion," someone said, "and died like a dog."

It was not going to be a good century for popes after all. The popes who followed Boniface did not have even his courage. They found it was more comfortable to live in Avignon, on the border of France, than in restless Rome. In Italy there was always strife and fighting. But here, on the banks of the Rhone River, life was quiet and undisturbed. A magnificent palace provided all the luxury a pope could wish; and around him lived the cardinals, his chief advisers, each one enjoying the wealth and pleasures of a prince. The French king was friendly now, with the pope under his power, and safe at Avignon the rulers of the Church still talked bravely about the great authority that Saint Peter had passed down to them. It was very pleasant there, and not for seventy years did any pope return to live at Rome.

But the popes of Avignon paid dearly for their peaceful life: for they lost the respect of Europe. It was through being bishop of Rome that a pope claimed to be head of the Church; and how could anyone really be bishop of Rome when he would not even live there? Angry complaints were heard about the money it took to keep up the pope's palace in royal style at Avignon. And because the Jews had once been exiled seventy years in Babylon, the years of comfort that the popes spent in a foreign place got the name of the "Babylonian captivity of the Church." For many hearts were heavy to see how the rulers of the Church had failed in their duty. Popes still had wealth and power and influence, but true honor was only for those who by strength of character could earn it.

Times indeed were changing. Here and there, in many countries, men were growing dissatisfied with the Church. It was not that they were tired of religion; what was wrong, they thought, was that the Church was not religious enough.

In Germany and in the Low Countries many people were struggling to find God. They wanted to know him in their hearts; they longed to live holy lives. To help one another they banded themselves into groups. Some called themselves Friends of God; others went by the name of Brethren of the Common Life. Their leaders preached to them in their own language; and they heard the gospel, not in the Latin tongue of the Church, which they did not understand, but in the speech they used in their homes and at their work. They did not leave the Church, and they did not mean to be disloyal to it, but their religion was different from what monks and priests and bishops stood for. Each soul wanted to know Christ for himself— not merely through going to Mass, and taking the sacraments, and obeying the rules that priests laid down, but through a new life stirring inside the human heart.

In England there arose a bold preacher whose name was John Wycliffe. Wycliffe despised all those who made an easy living out of the Church and gave nothing in return. He despised monks and friars who had grown lazy, who preferred to beg rather than work. He despised bishops who lived in luxury while the poor of the land could scarcely earn a livelihood. He taught that nobody had a right to rule others if he proved himself unfit to rule—not even though he were a king, not even if he were the pope himself. Popes, he said, have "no more right to excommunicate than devils have to curse." Wycliffe declared that if the pope and all his cardinals were thrown into hell, Christians would still be saved without them.

Those were dangerous words, but England was as safe a place as any in which to say them, for there was many an Englishman who was bitter about the money that the Church was taking from the country. One bishop had fifty estates of his own, and his time was largely spent in traveling from one to another, checking the accounts of his stewards. The Church claimed a tenth part of everything: the grain that grew in the fields, the poultry raised in the farmyards, the fish caught in the streams, the game killed in the forests. Much of the income went from England straight to Rome; and the popes appointed foreigners to the high positions in the English Church, giving their favorites the choicest places where they could grow rich from the earnings of the English people.

Wycliffe was called a heretic, but no one laid a hand upon him. He lived long enough to prepare a translation of the Bible into English; and he died peacefully in 1384. Long after his death the Church did to him what it could not do while he was alive: by order of the Church, his bones were dug up and burned, and thrown into the river.

They burned his books as well, but they did not burn them soon enough. Just as Wycliffe's ashes drifted downstream and into the measureless ocean, so did his ideas float across the sea and spread into Europe. Wycliffe had failed to reform the Church in England. But perhaps his words and his example would be of help to someone else in another time to come.

Lovely are the waters of Lake Constance, but John Hus had little time to look at them. From his prison cell he could see none of the beauty beyond the walls that separated him from the outside world. Day and night he lay in a dungeon built beside a sewer; and when he grew ill and feverish, his enemies came to question him, hoping to take advantage of his weakness.

Hus had not thought it would be this way. He had come to Constance, in 1414, with the emperor's guarantee of safe conduct. The emperor had pledged his word that Hus might safely enter the city and as safely leave again. Hus thought that the great Church council meeting in this German city would hear him while he defended his teachings. And the council would perhaps have heard him, if he had not insisted that the Holy Scriptures are higher than the Church. For the Council of

Constance was prepared to listen to criticism of the pope. The members believed that a Church council was superior to any pope; and, in fact, one reason for this meeting was to straighten out the pope's affairs and reform the evils of the Church.

But there was little sympathy at Constance with Hus or his opinions. To the council he was a troublemaker, who had stirred up the whole Bohemian nation—where Czechoslovakia now is—by his attacks on the evil lives of priests. Worse than that, he was a heretic. He had dared to disagree with the teachings of the Church. Indeed, it was known that he had read the books of Wycliffe, and approved of many things that the Englishman had written. As for the safe conduct, the Church held that a promise given to a heretic was not binding. If Hus was a heretic, he had no rights. If Hus imagined that he would be given a chance to explain his beliefs to the council, his enemies took the view that there was only one reason for summoning him to Constance: and that was to make him admit that he had been wrong. They would even make him, they decided, take back statements that he denied he ever made.

For many weary months the trial dragged on. From the dungeon Hus was transferred to a tower, where he was chained

to a post—by his hands in the daytime, by his hands and his feet at night. Only one of two things could happen: either Hus would confess his errors and ask pardon—and in that case he would be imprisoned for life—or else he might persist in his beliefs and die the death decreed for heretics. Hus knew how it must end. On June 10, 1415, he wrote a message "To the Whole Bohemian Nation":

> Faithful in God, men and women, rich and poor! I beg and entreat you to love the Lord God, praise his Word, gladly hear it and live according to it. Cling, I beg you, to the divine truth, which I have preached to you according to God's law.... I write this letter to you in prison and in fetters, expecting tomorrow the sentence of death, full of hope in God, resolved not to draw back from the divine truth.... How God has acted toward me, how he has been with me during all my troubles—that you will only know when by the grace of God we shall meet again in heaven.

In July the sentence was passed. Hus was dressed in the robes of a priest, and in his hands were placed the chalice to hold the wine of Holy Communion and the paten to hold the sacred bread. Then the robes were stripped from him, and the Communion cup and plate wrenched from his grasp. An archbishop said,

"O cursed Judas, who hast left the realms of peace and allied thyself with the Jews, we today take from thee the chalice of salvation."

Hus replied, "I hope this day to drink in the heavenly kingdom."

All the bishops then declared, "We consign thy soul to the devil."

Hus answered, "And I commit it to the most sacred Jesus Christ."

As a sign of mockery a high paper cap was placed on his head, and he was led outside the city. On the way the smell of smoke came to his nostrils. It was the smoke of his own books' being burned. As he reached the garden where the execution was to take place, Hus prayed aloud,

"Lord Jesus Christ, I will bear patiently and humbly this horrible, shameful, and cruel death for the sake of thy gospel and the preaching of thy Word."

Then he was stripped and tied to a stout pole. Someone noticed that he was facing the east—the direction in which lay the far-off Holy Land.

"Not that way!" was the shout. "He is a heretic—turn him to face the west!"

All was in readiness at last. The flame was applied to the wood, and straw was heaped high around the stake. The victim's lips moved in prayer, and then he began to sing a hymn. The wind blew the flames full in his face, and John Hus sang no more on earth. Another reformer had paid the price of putting Scripture above the commands of pope or council.

Two centuries had gone by since Boniface VIII had died so badly. The dust of Wycliffe and Hus and many another fighter for the truth had long since returned to the earth. The popes were back in Rome, and happy to be there.

It was not a peaceful life; for Italy was torn by civil war, and a pope had to be cunning to keep his life, let alone retain his high position. But it was good nevertheless to be alive in Italy at that time. For the age of the New Learning had arrived. Scholars were busy discovering ancient manuscripts. Poets and writers were hard at work. Famous painters and sculptors and architects were flourishing in those golden days. How long ago seemed the age of the barbarians! The pope had at his personal service two of the greatest artists of all time—Michelangelo and Raphael. One pope set out to cover the walls of his rooms with paintings, to rebuild St. Peter's Church, and to create for himself the most magnificent tomb that the genius of Italy could design.

In 1513, Leo X became pope. He well appreciated the opportunity to surround himself with the artists and architects and writers whose work and company he found so pleasant. "The papacy is ours," he said to his brother. "Let us enjoy it!" One must, of course, be careful. Leo appointed an armed guard to protect him when he was at Mass, for fear, while he knelt at the altar, a rival might stab him in the back. But to be pope was worth the risk.

Never was there such a festival as that to celebrate Leo's enthronement as pope. In every street and house of Rome decorations adorned the city. The rich brought out their treasures of ancient Greek and Roman art. In honor of the new head of Christ's Church, statues of pagan gods were proudly displayed. It was a gay time to be pope in Rome.

It was pleasant, but of course it also was expensive. There were rumors that in foreign countries men resented having to pay so much for the pope's personal enjoyment. One warning came, which Pope Leo might have heeded as a ship's captain heeds a hurricane signal. The pope's own messenger in Germany wrote to him that there was discontent in that land. "In Germany," he wrote, "they are only waiting until some fellow once opens his mouth against Rome."

But who would be the "fellow"? Who would dare to open his mouth against Rome? The problem was not what people thought in Germany, but how to get more money. Leo ordered a new tax on the German Church.

That was in 1516. Not guessing what another year might bring, the pope thought happily that all was well.

$\mathcal{P}art\ III$

THE CHURCH SHAKES
THE WORLD

CHAPTER 11

THUNDERBOLTS

EVERYBODY was afraid of hell, but hardly anyone really expected to go there. Hell was for the very wicked, for heretics, for sinners who died without repenting. The ordinary man, who went to Mass, and confessed his sins, and obeyed the priest, did not think that he would be sent to everlasting torment.

The average person expected to get to heaven; but he also imagined that he would have to wait awhile. Saints might go there directly when they died; but saints were few and far between. For all the rest, there must be some kind of punishment for sin. Most people, the Church taught, would at death go into a place called *purgatory*. There they would be purged of their sins. There they would be cleansed by suffering: and the suffering would be like that of the damned souls in hell, only it would not go on forever. In a vision a poet dreamed that already he was walking through the fires of purgatory. How gladly he would have thrown himself, he cried, into a pool of molten glass, to cool his body from the heat of those dread flames!! But when a soul had suffered long enough, he could pass on to the joy and peace of paradise.

This, then, was the prospect of what awaited a man at death; and it was enough to frighten many into a decent life, so that the pains of purgatory might not last so long. But the Roman Church, which taught its people to tremble at these things, also offered to make the way through purgatory a little easier. The good deeds of Christ and the saints had won them more reward than they needed for themselves: they could share it with sinful men. It was like a treasure house—the treasury of merit, it was named—and the pope or his officials could draw upon it as upon a bank account. Men could obtain an *indulgence*, which was a certificate that they had been granted a share in this divine treasury of goodness. That would shorten the time of a soul in purgatory, or perhaps allow one to go to heaven without any punishment at all.

But an indulgence must be eamed. Some earned it by fighting in a crusade, or by journeying to Rome in a year of jubilee. The simplest way was just to buy it, if one had the price. If a person had already gained an indulgence for himself, there was nothing to prevent him from buying another to help the poor soul of a friend or loved one who had died and gone into the flames of purgatory. The money was useful to the Church, and the indulgences brought comfort to the people. The sellers did not always make it clear that the indulgences released one only from penances that priests had set—not from the guilt itself. The ignorant sometimes thought that their way was now paid to heaven, and they need worry no more about their sins.

But there were others who were not satisfied to buy God's mercy for a sum of money. It was their sins that troubled them, and not merely the fear of punishment. They wanted to be pure in the sight of God, and they would not wait until death to cleanse themselves. Some of these took their anxious spirits into monasteries, away from the sins and temptations of the world. Some of them, having dedicated themselves as monks, fasted, and kept watch by night, and prayed continually to Christ, to Mary, and to the saints. In the monasteries some tortured themselves, as if to undergo a purgatory upon earth, hoping by the suffering of their bodies to purge their souls.

And in the monasteries many found at last the peace for which they longed.

On July 2, 1505, a young German student named Martin Luther was traveling from his home to the university at Erfurt. For several months he had been troubled about the state of his soul, wondering what would become of him at the Last Judgment. On this day it seemed to him for a moment that the time had come to face his Maker. For a violent thunderstorm broke about him while he still had miles to go. A bolt of lightning struck so near that he was thrown breathless to the ground.

Luther was terrified, as anyone would have been; and like a man of his time he cried to a saint to help him: "Saint Anna, save me!" And fearing that prayer was not enough, he added a vow: if his life were spared, he would become a monk.

He was not the first man to make a rash vow when his life was in danger; and, like many others, he wished when the danger was over that he had not gone so far. This was not what he had intended to do at all! Certainly his father —a miner who hoped to see his son grow rich as a lawyer —would be displeased. But a vow was a vow. Luther was afraid to go back upon his word.

His family warned him that if he refused to study law and became a monk, he would no longer be welcome at his home. Nevertheless, Luther held a farewell supper and said good-by to his friends. It was good-by, not only to them, but to all the outside world. It must be left behind, when he sadly made his way to a monastery with the forbidding name of "The Black Cloister." Perhaps, at any rate, he would be able to overcome his sins. As he was received into the monastery, the monks joined in the customary prayer for their new brother:

> O Lord, make worthy of thy blessing this thy servant whom we have just clothed in the habit of a monk, and grant that he may thereby win eternal life through Jesus Christ our Lord.

It was a very different life from what he had known before. Like every other monk, he had to learn to walk with his head bowed and his eyes looking down. The young student who had once been gay must give up laughing now. He must do lowly work in the kitchen, and go out begging. His little room was poorly furnished: he had a chair, a table, a bed with straw mattress and woolen blankets, and a candlestick. He must read the Latin Bible daily, and once a week he must confess all his sins to a priest. After a year of trial, Luther was allowed to make the vows by which he forever became a monk: there was no retreating now. In 1507 he was ordained a priest; and for the first time he stood before the altar to officiate at the Mass, uttering the sacred words at which the bread and wine, as the Church believed, were turned into the real body and blood of Christ. To celebrate this occasion there was a feast; and even Martin's father, who had partly forgiven him, attended. Hard study brought the new priest to the place where he was permitted to give lectures. The young man whose father had meant him to be a lawyer had become a teacher of theology.

Luther was doing well in his new profession, but his life was little different from that of many other monks. It was a pleasant break in routine when he got the chance to visit Rome in 1510. Overcome by excitement as the great city came into view, he threw himself to the ground, crying out, "Blessed be thou, holy Rome!"

The visit, however, was not without its disappointments. His earnest soul was shocked to find that too many of the Italian priests were not so religious as the priests of Germany. Their wish seemed to be to get through Mass as quickly as they could. Shocking too were the stories of crime and filthy life among the common people—even here in Rome! Nor were all the popes, he was told, altogether pure and good. It was distressing to learn such things. Yet, being a faithful Roman Catholic priest, he could not fail to be thrilled by his experiences in the ancient capital of the Church. There were world-famous shrines to see, and altars at which a priest might say Mass and know that he had freed a suffering soul from purgatory. Luther gazed in amazement at the many relics on display: a thick rope said to have been the one with which Judas Iscariot hanged himself, paintings believed to have come from the hand of Saint Luke. Precious to Luther was his visit to the catacombs: he could not have enough of the underground graves where countless martyrs of ancient times were buried.

But Luther could not stay forever among these awe-inspiring sights. Duty called him home. He had his work to do as a preacher and professor at the University of Wittenberg.

Wittenberg was no great place in which to live. It was, in fact, a small and ugly town, full of wooden houses begrimed with smoke. Even the tower room he had for his study was too small for comfort. Luther, however, was not thinking of outward things so much as of his soul within. He had hoped to find peace from his sins in the life of the monastery; and he had not found it.

He could not understand it. He lived like other monks; but they found the joy of feeling their sins forgiven, and Luther did not. Perhaps he was not trying hard enough. He fasted more and more; he kept himself from the sleep his body craved; but, although he ruined his health by his self-discipline, still he found no rest for his troubled mind. His sins haunted him by day and by night. The fear of hell took hold of him, and he wondered if he were damned. He read the Bible constantly, but what he read there only made him feel more strongly God's righteousness and his own wretched sinfulness. He repented of his sins as best he knew how, but never believing that he was really pardoned.

It was in the spring of 1513 that he saw his mistake. "It was as if the gates swung open," he wrote, "and I entered into paradise." The gates swung slowly, but he could see the light ahead. He had found the answer he had so long been seeking.

How mistaken he had been, to think that he could make himself good in God's eyes by the things he did to win reward! To go without meals and sleep, to punish one's body—what would that gain him, in his battle with his sins? Nobody could earn the approval of God. All men are sinners, and the enemies of God, and no man could hope to save his own soul. But God had solved the problem of man's sin. For our God is a God of mercy, in Christ freely forgiving those who trust his promises. A verse of Scripture rang like a bell in Luther's mind: "The just shall live by faith." By faith! Faith in God—not the endless doing of good works which got one nowhere—was what was asked of men. That was the way of peace.

Eagerly he turned again to the Bible. Now it did not frighten him, but it rather reassured him: for everything he read told him he was right. The burden began to roll away from his heavy heart. Now it was a joyful thing to be a priest, a preacher, and a teacher: for now he had good news to tell. What he had discovered was the real message of the Scriptures and the Church.

And while he was reflecting upon the joyous truth that he had found, and telling it to others, news came that a man named John Tetzel had arrived in Germany to sell indulgences. This was in the year 1517, four years after Luther had first made his great discovery. He had had time enough to think about his message, and it was very different from the reports of Tetzel's sermons that came to Luther's ears.

To his superstitious audiences Tetzel was shouting:

> Do you not hear your dead parents crying out: "Have mercy upon us. We are in sore pain and you can set us free for a mere pittance. We have borne you, we have trained you and educated you, we have left you all our property, and you are so hardhearted and cruel, that you leave us to roast in the flames when you could so easily release us!"

And his eloquence was rewarded. The people were crowding forward at his meetings to buy the indulgences he had to sell. Tetzel assured them it was a good bargain. "The soul flies out of purgatory," he declared, "when the money clinks in the box!"

Luther could not bear it. The time had come to speak. Was this the gospel of Jesus Christ? But then there was the question—how should he make his voice heard? There was one way which professors sometimes used. It was their custom to publish a list of theses, or points for argument, and challenge anyone who wished to dispute these opinions to a public debate. Seldom did anything come of it, but it was worth trying. At least Luther would have made known his beliefs about indulgences.

He drew up ninety-five points for dispute. He might not be right about them all: but if other scholars would debate them, the truth might be discovered. In his list of theses, Luther declared that no one can truly repent of sin by simply going to a priest and making a bargain: real repentance must go on throughout the whole of the Christian's life on earth. Only God can do away with the punishment of guilt. Not even the pope can help a soul in purgatory, for he has no power over the dead. A repentant man needs no indulgence, for, if he feels remorse for his sins, he is forgiven already. Besides, if the pope could save souls from purgatory, why does he not do so out of Christian love and not for the sake of money?

The *Ninety-five Theses* were printed on a card. On October 31, 1517, at twelve noon, Martin Luther walked to the Castle Church in Wittenberg, carrying his placard. It was the work of a moment to post it on the church door.

Along the road that he had walked he returned. Behind him a little patch of white stood out against the darker wood of the door. Luther did not know what he had done. He did not know that because of that placard the Church would never be the same again. He did not know that this date would go down in history as Reformation Day.

He was just a monk, a professor of theology, who had offered to take part in a debate among other scholars.

Within three months almost the whole of Germany knew about that placard. The printing press, newly invented, spread copies throughout the land. Everyone was talking about Luther's *Ninety-five Theses*. Even laymen, with no training in theology, eagerly read Luther's proclamation. "There is a man who will do something!" someone exclaimed. Luther was not yet sure of the truth of what he had written. But readers all over Germany accepted it without question; and defenders of indulgences leaped into the discussion, eager to answer back.

In Rome the matter came to the ears of Pope Leo X. He dismissed it with a wave of the hand. "A squabble among monks!" he said. It was reported to Luther that Leo added: "A drunken German wrote it. He will think differently when he is sober!"

But the "drunken German" was finding friends. There was, for one, the young Philip Melanchthon, at the age of twenty-one professor of Greek at Wittenberg. He was delicate and cautious and gentle—the very opposite of Luther, who was so passionate, so reckless, sometimes so rude of speech. But the younger man attached himself to the older for the sake of truth; and in the future he would prove a good friend and faithful ally. Already he was spreading Luther's fame among his fellow scholars. Everyone who longed to be free of the ancient superstitions and the newer evils of the Church was watching Luther with interest. Even the great Erasmus of Rotterdam—the most famous scholar of his time, the man who had published the New Testament in the original Greek, and who had more than once delighted to poke fun at monks and priests — was filled with admiration.

Another friend that Luther won was the Elector Frederick, the prince who ruled the German state of Saxony. He too was convinced that Luther was right; and one day he would prove his friendship when Luther badly needed it.

The people of Germany were also rallying in large numbers to Luther's side in the great dispute. That was what alarmed the Church. It might have started as a mere "squabble among monks," but the fact remained that the people were not buying so many indulgences as before. Something must be done. If Luther would not submit to threats, perhaps he might be bribed. One zealous scholar thought that he would make Luther ridiculous by defeating him in a public argument. And that is where he made his mistake. For it was not until Dr. Eck had won this debate that Luther realized how far he had strayed from the Roman Church.

Dr. Eck was skilled in the art of disputing. At the great

debate in Leipzig he set out to prove that Luther was rebelling against the Roman Church. This had not occurred to Luther. He had thought that he was only doing his duty as a priest and a professor. But Dr. Eck was clever. "You are really a follower of John Hus," he declared. Luther jumped to his feet, angrily to deny the charge. But not so fast—perhaps Eck in a way was right. Luther's friends listened in horror, while he publicly acknowledged that there was much in the teaching of Hus that as a Christian he could not deny.

Dr. Eck saw his triumph. Hus was a condemned heretic. Luther was opposing all the authority and the wisdom of the holy Church. What did he have to put in its place? Only his own conscience! He had nothing to support him except his own opinions! The man who refused to accept the decisions of the pope was a rebel against the Church.

Luther left the debating hall a changed man. He was in revolt against the Roman Church, and at last he knew it. He must go the whole way now. Boldly he called the pope a tyrant, with no right to interfere in the affairs of any nation. He declared that there was no such thing as a special class of priests: all men, according to the Scriptures, were priests to one another. Nor was there any reason for men or women to go to monasteries, in order to serve God better than others, for everyone could serve God by doing his daily tasks in love and joyfulness. "What you do in your homes," said Luther, "is

worth as much as if you did it up in heaven for our Lord God." Every Christian, he said, was a free man, and need not obey the demands for fasting and pilgrimages that the Church imposed. Yet being free did not mean doing what you might please: it meant being a servant to other men in the daily walks of life. As for the Roman teaching that at the Mass the bread and wine turned into the body and blood of Christ, it was a superstition and a lie. There were, furthermore, no sacraments except what Jesus Christ himself commanded in the gospel, no matter what the Church might say.

On and on the stream of Luther's teaching flowed. Caution was thrown to the winds. Enemies might compare him to Mohammed, but still he would speak. His books might be burned, but he would write more. He would spare himself no risk to preach the gospel. And while half of Germany reviled him, the other half was cheering.

Even Pope Leo X, so slow to take alarm, knew that the mouth of this heretic must be stopped. There was a way. Had it not always worked before? He would issue a bull— a solemn decree from the pope himself—declaring Luther's teaching an abominable heresy. Luther would have his chance to retract his statements; and if he failed to do so, there would be excommunication, and then, no doubt, condemnation, the sentence of death, the fiery death of heretics.

Pacing up and down his hunting lodge, while his companions were giving chase to wild boars, Leo planned the language of his decree: "Arise, O Lord, and defend thine own cause.... A wild boar seeks to destroy thy vineyard."

Late in 1520, the papal bull was delivered to Germany. Luther had sixty days to withdraw his teachings and submit to the pope. If he persisted in his heresies, excommunication would follow.

Sixty days? The pope did not need to wait so long for an answer.

On December 10, 1520, word went around Wittenberg that there would be that night a bonfire such as had never been seen before.

CHAPTER 12

THE REFORMATION TAKES ROOT

THE notice of the bonfire was posted in public view. It read:

"All who hold to the truth of the gospel are invited to be present at nine o'clock at the Chapel of the Holy Cross outside the walls, where the impious books of papal law and scholastic theology will be burned according to ancient and apostolic custom."

Excitement was running high throughout Wittenberg. It was a common enough sight to see the books of heretics piled up and set ablaze. Luther's own books were being burned at the order of the Church all across Germany. But this time it was the writings of the great theological scholars of the past that were condemned to the flames. And that was not all. The books of papal law, the books containing the decrees of pope and Church councils by which the everyday life of Europe had long been ruled—they were to vanish in smoke! It promised to be a historic evening. Who could tell what might come of it?

At the time arranged, Luther made his appearance at the city gate. At the last moment, someone thrust into his hand a booklet which he grasped tightly. The fire was lighted, and professors and students began to heap books upon the blaze. Luther stepped forward, praying, and trembling with emotion. In a voice that could scarcely be heard, he said:

"Because thou hast brought down the truth of God, may the Lord today bring thee down into this fire!"

His hand shot forward. The booklet he had been clutching dropped into the flames.

The spectators did not know what was in the booklet. But Luther knew. It was the papal bull of Leo X, declaring him a heretic, calling upon him to repent or suffer the penalties of the Church. Luther had made his final decision. He was an avowed enemy of Rome.

The bonfire was over in ten minutes. But news of what had happened at the gates of Wittenberg ran swiftly through the land. Luther had thrown off the shackles of Roman law. He had hurled the pope's challenge back in his teeth. Two months later the messenger of the pope was reporting at Rome:

"The whole of Germany is in full revolt. Nine tenths raise the war cry, 'Luther!' The watchword of the other tenth who do not care about Luther is 'Death to the Roman Court!'"

To Luther the wave of victory was God's victory. The pope, he said, was Antichrist, and the Word of God was smiting him.

"Have I not," he wrote, "succeeded in taking more from the pope, the bishops, the priests, and the monks with my mouth alone, without striking a blow, than have all the emperors, kings, and princes with all their force? Why? Because, as Saint Paul says, the Antichrist shall be destroyed out of the mouth of Christ. It is not our work that is now going on in the world, for man alone could not begin or carry through such a thing. It is Another who is driving the wheel, One whom the Papists do not see."

Germany was indeed in a turmoil. It was the words of Luther's mouth that had started it, but there were many patriotic Germans who were determined to finish the fight against Rome—by force if necessary. Fiery knights and nobles put themselves on Luther's side. The older scholars like Erasmus, who had prepared the way for the attack on superstitions, were growing alarmed by the new movement. It was too violent for their taste. But it was too late to stop it now.

The new head of the Holy Roman Empire, Charles V of Spain, intended to try. As the ruler of vast dominions, he had other problems besides the Reformation movement in Germany. He had, in fact, his own troubles with the pope. Besides, the princes of the states in Germany could be very independent; the emperor might be in theory their head, but it was another thing to rule them in practice. Nevertheless, as emperor and as a loyal servant of his Church, Charles felt in duty bound to crush the German revolt against the power of Rome.

In 1521 the opportunity seemed to have come. There was to be an imperial diet, or assembly of rulers, at the German city of Worms. The pope wrote to Charles, urging him to have a decree proclaimed that would condemn Luther according to the laws of the Empire. Charles imagined that he would be able to persuade the diet to declare Luther an outlaw.

But when the Diet of Worms met, the German princes were not ready to move so quickly. They knew too well the tyranny of Rome over Germany not to appreciate the value of Luther. The Elector Frederick of Saxony, along with others, insisted that Luther should not be condemned without a hearing. Now the emperor was in a quandary. The last thing he desired was Luther's presence at Worms. There ought to be no controversy or debate: Luther should simply be condemned. But it was clear that he would never get the consent of the assembly unless Luther were first summoned to appear. Regretfully he gave the order that the Reformer should come to Worms, and that he should be guaranteed safe conduct there and home again.

Luther was joyful on receiving the summons, but his friends were fearful. Of what value had a guarantee of safe conduct been, they pointed out, to Hus? Had Hus not been burned at the stake, despite all the fair promises he had received?

Luther retorted:

"Hus has been burned, but not the truth with him. I will go to Worms, though as many devils were aiming at me as there are tiles on the roof.... He lives and reigns who preserved the three children in the furnace of the Babylonian king. If he is unwilling to preserve me, my life is a small thing compared with Christ's, who was wickedly slain to the disgrace of all and the harm of many!"

Luther's journey to the diet was something of a triumphal march. Who was not eager to catch a glimpse of the Reformer— perhaps going to his doom? When, on April 16, he reached Worms, his arrival was announced by the blast of a trumpet. Though it was mealtime, the whole town poured out into the streets to see him.

The next day, in the bishop's palace, Luther made his appearance before all the leading princes of the Holy Roman Empire. The emperor wanted to get it over quickly. The titles of twenty books were read to him. Had he written these? Yes, he had written them—and many more besides! Would he take back what he had written in these books? As to that, he said, he wanted more time to think before he gave his reply.

The emperor frowned, and Luther's enemies at the diet were displeased. There was, after all, going to be a prolonged debate. However, his request for time could not very well be refused, and he was given until the following day to make his answer.

All night long Luther was in consultation with his friends— yet taking time to visit the bedside of a dying man. When the time came for his next hearing before the majestic diet, he was prepared.

Luther began his speech by dividing his writings into three groups. The first were about faith and morals, and in these there could surely be no harm or crime. The second were attacks on the pope. How could he withdraw these? Could he possibly consent to the pope's abominable tyranny over the souls of men? The third group consisted of attacks on various individuals; and in these, he granted, he had sometimes spoken too violently. He must, however, be condemned clearly by the teachings of the Bible. Unless he could be persuaded by "Scripture and righteousness," he said, "I cannot and I will not revoke anything, for it is neither safe nor right to act against conscience. God help me. Amen."

His enemies were furious. Yet they did not dare to condemn him without at least trying to persuade him of his error. The discussions dragged on for weeks. The time of the safe conduct was coming toward its end. Already some were urging Charles to arrest Luther, as Hus had been arrested, on the ground that one does not need to keep promises made to heretics. It was time for Luther to be away.

On the journey back, Luther was suddenly surrounded by a party of armed men. They led him away from the public road, into a forest. By twisting, half-hidden trails through the woods they brought him, late at night, to the foot of an ancient castle. Huge and imposing, dark among dark trees, it loomed up on the hill above him.

It was a castle of Elector Frederick of Saxony. Luther was among friends.

When the delegates to the diet had already begun to leave, a decree was rushed through condemning Luther. If he could be found, he would be subject to the penalty of death. Rumors went abroad that Luther was already dead.

But letters to his friends soon reassured them. They were dated merely "from the Region of Birds." But Luther was safe enough, in the Castle of the Wartburg.

For nearly a year Luther remained hidden at the Wartburg. Even the elector of Saxony would not risk letting him be seen

abroad in his own territories. There was plenty to do, even in seclusion. Luther set about translating the Bible into German, and in three months had finished the New Testament. The gospel could now be read by the common people, in the everyday language that Luther knew so well.

But Luther was not the man to stay long in hiding— not, especially, when news came of troubles at Wittenberg. Men who called themselves prophets were preaching there, claiming that they had been inspired directly by God. They were denouncing education, teaching that only work done with one's hands was worthy in God's sight. Every custom of the Church that resembled the practices of the Roman Church was condemned. Luther was horrified at the extreme doctrines of these new reformers. The elector begged him to remain safely at the Wartburg. But Luther was not anxious for his own safety. He was needed at Wittenberg.

To the place where the Reformation had begun he now returned—never again to leave it for long at a time. Back at Wittenberg, he opposed the prophets. There was no need to overturn the whole Church and forsake all its ancient customs. The task, he taught, was not to make a new Church but to reform the old. And the gospel, he insisted, was not helped by war or social revolution: the preacher must simply trust in the power of God's Word.

He won his battle with the prophets at Wittenberg; but the movement he had started was getting out of his hands. He could not control what was happening in the length and breadth of Germany. In 1524 disaster struck. The peasants revolted against their masters. It was not right, they declared, that those whom Christ had made free should be in bondage to men. In their struggle for liberty they looked to Luther for support. Was it not he who had taught them to believe in freedom?

It was a hard decision for Luther. He knew well enough how bitter was the lot of the poor peasant, how cruelly the helpless folk of the land were abused by their masters. But to rise up in rebellion against all law and order—no, he could not sanction that! God had given power to the government to rule the people, and the duty of the people was to obey. The Christian must not defend himself by force: force is the weapon of the government, and the Christian must use the sword only to carry out the orders of the ruler. The peasants expected Luther's help; instead, he called upon the nobles to cut down and destroy the rebellious peasants without pity.

They never forgave him. The ferocious acts of the rebels were repaid many times over by the nobles, who were only too glad to follow Luther's advice. Had Luther supported the other side, the Reformer would have been blamed for the revolt. Nobles and princes would have turned against the Church of the Reformation, and no one knows what the consequences might have been. As it was, the poor of the country were driven away from the Reformer's side, and their enthusiasm for his cause turned to hatred and to bitterness.

No matter what decision Luther made in the Peasants' Revolt, there could be only one result that was certain: calamity for Germany and for the Church.

From that time on, discouragements came thick and fast. Amidst them all Luther looked for happiness in marriage, and found it. There was even trouble about that. For his wife, Katharina von Bora, had been a nun. The thought of Luther, a former monk, marrying a nun, shocked the Reformer's friends. "The whole world will laugh at you!" they exclaimed. But Luther was determined, not only to have the joy of marriage, but also to show the world— whether it laughed or not—that the ministers of his Church were at liberty to take wives as did other men.

It was good that Luther now had a home in which to relax, for his troubles were increasing. He quarreled with the great scholar Erasmus: in the eyes of Erasmus, Luther was a barbarian; and to Luther, Erasmus was a heathen. More serious still, he quarreled with Ulrich Zwingli, the brave Swiss patriot who pioneered the Reformation in his native land. To Luther it seemed that Zwingli was teaching that the Lord's Supper was nothing more than a feast held in memory of Christ, and that

Christ was not really present at the Table. Luther held that though the Roman Catholics were mistaken in believing that the bread and wine were by the priest's words turned into the body and blood of the Lord, yet Christ was in reality present in the food that was taken at the sacred Supper. Desperately the leaders of the Reformation sought to get the two men to agree; but when Luther and Zwingli met for a conference at Marburg, Luther declared that he would not argue. "This is my body," Christ had said; and Luther would listen to no other interpretation of those words than his own. Zwingli offered the German Reformer the right hand of fellowship, but Luther would not take it. Because of this dispute the Church in Germany was to be divided from the Church in Switzerland for centuries to come.

In Germany itself things could have been going better. The country was made up of many states, each with a ruler of its own. Not all the princes were on the side of the Reformation. The most that could apparently be hoped for was that in states ruled by Lutherans the Reformation would go forward; while in the others there was no choice but to see the Roman Catholic Church continue. The Reformers were not even sure of getting as good a bargain as that. In 1529, when the Roman Catholic party in Germany was winning, a decree was issued forbidding the Reformation to progress any farther in states that had not accepted it, while Roman Catholics were to be at perfect liberty in Lutheran states. In vain did the Lutherans demand a General Council of the Church to consider the dispute. The Lutheran princes made a *protest*: and that protest gave the Church of the Reformation the name it was to have ever after—the name of *Protestant*.

The Reformers could not always be happy even about the Lutheran princes. Some, like Elector Frederick of Saxony, were certainly sincere. But others had become Lutheran in order to follow the wishes of their people, or because they hoped to be on the winning side. Some had supported the Reformation because they were angry at the evils of the old Church, and its methods of taking money from Germany to Rome. Others still looked greedily upon the property of the Roman Church, and became Protestants in order to make that property their own.

The Reformation, however, had come to stay. Already the Protestant doctrines had found their way into France, where a heroic few were defying the wrath of their Roman Catholic rulers and neighbors. The Lutheran Church was moving north into Denmark, Norway, and Sweden, and soon it would take possession of those kingdoms. For a time the Reformation was to hold sway in Poland and in Hungary, until the Roman Church became strong enough again to cast it out.

Meanwhile in Germany the Protestant faith was advancing to the sound of immortal music. Luther's great battle hymn rang through the land:

> A safe stronghold our God is still,
>   A trusty shield and weapon;
> He'll help us clear from all the ill
>   That hath us now o'ertaken....
>
> And, though they take our life,
>   Goods, honor, children, wife,
>   Yet is their profit small;
>   These things shall vanish all;
> The city of God remaineth.

Melanchthon the scholar was busy setting down in orderly fashion the teachings of the Reformation faith. Through the whole scene moved Luther—laughing with his friends, playing with his children, blasting out in anger against his foes, writing countless books and pamphlets, preaching innumerable sermons full of tenderness and joy and hope.

It was only his faith in God's Word that kept him going. He was growing weary, and his body was racked with pain and sickness. He was worried about the Reformation: it had not turned out so well as he had hoped, and the times, he thought, had grown more wicked. Yet God was faithful! God was to be trusted! From his melancholy he roused himself ever and again to proclaim the faith by which he lived.

Rest came to him at last, on February 18, 1546. In the town

where he was born he closed his eyes and did not open them again. His body was carried back to Wittenberg; and in the church on whose door he had posted the *Ninety-five Theses* almost thirty years before, his body was laid away. There he was joined in 1560 by his faithful friend Melanchthon, the remains of the two Reformers resting together within the same church walls.

Things were going to be worse in Germany than even Luther dreamed. Not for over a hundred years after the Reformer's death would the unhappy land find any settled peace: and then it would be the peace of an exhausted and ruined country. From 1618 to 1648, Germany was doomed to be the battle ground of such a war as this world has seldom seen. Ruthless and ambitious men would mix religion with their other motives, to fight one another until none could fight any longer.

At the end of it all, Germany had its first taste of tolerance in religion. The Protestant and Roman Catholic Churches became equal. The age of religious warfare was passing away at last. But who could reckon up the cost? More than a quarter of the population of Germany had perished, some by the ferocious cruelty of armies, others by disease and famine. Fields once fertile and smiling were empty of crops or cattle. Having suffered too long from violence, the common people cared for neither the laws of man nor the love of God.

Yet amidst the ruin the Lutheran faith still sang its song. Still there was trust in God, and joy, and thankfulness. Hardly able to find bread or clothes for his own children, Martin Rinkart sat down and wrote:

> Now thank we all our God
> With heart and hands and voices,
> Who wondrous things hath done,
> In whom His world rejoices;
> Who, from our mothers' arms,
> Hath blessed us on our way
> With countless gifts of love,
> And still is ours today.

CHAPTER 13

OPPOSING FORCES

O N a July night in 1536 two Frenchmen were engaged in violent argument in a Geneva inn.

Each had made a name for himself as a campaigner for the Protestant faith; and both had had to flee for their lives from their native land. There the resemblance seemed to cease. William Farel was middle-aged, brawny, and gifted with a mighty voice that could shout down a multitude. The other man was twenty years younger. He was thin, pale, timid, and sickly. His name was John Calvin.

Farel had not meant to speak so loudly. He had set out to explain what had happened in this Swiss city, and how much Calvin was needed there. The people of Geneva had thrown off the yoke of their Roman Catholic bishop and had voted to become Protestant. But it was a wild and immoral city. The task of ministering to these souls was too much for Farel singlehanded. Would not Calvin stay and help?

Farel knew the quality of the man who was sitting with him in the room. Frail though Calvin might be, and afraid of physical danger, he was strong when strength was needed. He had given up comfort in France, and a brilliant career as a lawyer, because it had come to him that he must throw himself wholly on the mercy of Christ and devote his life to the work of the Protestant ministry. Forsaking everything for the sake of his new faith, he had, in peril of his life, celebrated Holy Communion in hidden caves where the victims of persecution gathered. He had preached to Italian peasants, and been driven away by stones. Only twenty-seven years old, already he had written a great book which would become more famous still as all Europe came to know of it—the *Institutes of the Christian Religion*. Farel coveted for Geneva the razor-sharp mind of Calvin, his polished pen, his immense devotion to the truth.

But Calvin was saying no. Nothing appealed to him less than to stay in Geneva. He had not intended to come here at all; only the fact that a war was raging along the road he meant to take had caused him to visit the Swiss city, and his plan was to accept a night's lodging and then journey on to Strasbourg. There he would be able to continue his studies and his writing in the quietness he so much desired. He was not, he said, in any way fitted to do the work in Geneva. He was sick; and besides, he was far too ill-tempered to be the pastor of a congregation.

"In the name of the Lord," cried Calvin, "have pity on me and let me serve God in some other way!"

It was then that Farel lost his self-control. His voice shook the room.

"And I," he shouted, "in the name of Almighty God say to you: your studies are a mere excuse! If you refuse to dedicate yourself here with us to this work of God, God will curse you, for you seek yourself rather than Christ!"

Calvin was stricken with terror. The curse of God! He dared not resist the command of the Lord. Overpowered by a will higher than his own, he surrendered. He would stay to minister to the Church in Geneva. Perhaps it would have been safer to risk a merciful bullet in his heart, along the war-torn road he had meant to travel, than to endure the trials that might be waiting for him in this place. But God had called him here, and from God's commandment there was no escape.

The city was as bad as Farel had painted it. In Calvin's opinion it was, in fact, worse. Calvin had long been noted for the strictness of his life. What he saw in Geneva shocked him, sickened him. The people had won liberty, and did not know how to use it. Gambling, drunkenness, and immorality were everywhere. The ladies and gentlemen of the city delighted more in indecent clothes than in religion. To dancing and games of cards in moderation Calvin would not object; but in Geneva how few there were who thought of anything but pleasure!

Calvin had not become a pastor here in order to stand by while the people drank and danced themselves to ruin. It was the pastor's duty to teach the truth and to demand obedience to the laws of God. And it was, Calvin insisted, the duty of the government to enforce God's law. On one point above all he would not yield. Those who proved themselves rebellious against the gospel must not be allowed to sit at the Lord's Table. It was necessary, he said, "that all manifest idolaters, blasphemers, assassins, thieves, rakes, false witnesses, seditious and quarrelsome men, brawlers, drunkards, prodigals, after having been warned, if they do not mend their ways, should be deprived of the communion of the faithful until they had repented."

The man in the street at first was filled with admiration for this preacher. Here was a minister who made no difference between rich and poor, high and low. The story went around that an important man defended his misconduct on the ground that he had fought for the liberty of the city. Calvin answered sternly, "It is the act of a bad citizen, when he has shed his blood for his country, to claim as a reward the right to sin and to set a bad example!"

But Calvin's popularity could not last for long. It was true that he made no distinction between rich and poor, but that meant that the poor too began to suffer under the Frenchman's iron discipline. Crowds began to mutter threats. A party which later came to be known as the Libertines, led by prominent citizens and supported by most of the city, set itself up in opposition to Calvin and Farel. Soon the Libertines had gained control of the city government. The climax came on Easter, 1538.

The government ordered the two French pastors to give Communion in a manner to which Calvin and Farel were opposed. Their answer was they would give no Communion at all that Easter. The government then forbade them to preach.

On Saturday night, crowds rioted in the streets, keeping Calvin wakeful on his bed. In the morning the multitude were still shouting. There was talk of throwing Calvin into the river. It would be a bold act to venture outside his house, much less go to his church, that day.

And into that crowd on Easter morning Calvin went— the timid, shrinking Calvin, who could not bear the sound of a gun. Friends shielded him from the throng while he made his way to his church. He stood up in the pulpit before the angry congregation, and saw guns and swords being waved above the people's heads. And standing there he denounced the sins of the city, declared that the congregation was unfit to take its place at the Lord's Table, and departed without giving Communion to anyone. Farel had meanwhile fought through the crowds to reach the pulpit of his own church in the city. To the same kind of audience that Calvin faced, Farel shouted: "I will not dispense the Lord's Supper. . . . Where did you spend last night?"

The pastors left their churches as they had come, amidst howling mobs. No one laid a hand upon them. But the next day the government met, and gave them three days to leave the city.

What a release this was! Now Calvin could continue his interrupted journey. A few months later, a little church of French Protestants at Strasbourg called him to be its pastor. Now he could relax a little. There were troubles waiting for him in Strasbourg too, but also more happiness than he had known. He could find some peace, listening to his congregation singing to simple and lovely airs the psalms he loved so well. And in Strasbourg he was to find the comfort of a happy marriage. The hideous experiences of Geneva were over.

Three years later Calvin was on his way back to Geneva. The city that could not live with him had discovered that it also could not live without him. The people needed a firm hand at the helm. Without the leadership of Calvin, Geneva feared that it would soon fall again under the power of the Roman Church. A deputation from the government visited him at Strasbourg, to beg him to return.

Calvin heard the summons with horror. Must he go back to that hateful place and plunge once more into the struggle that had all but killed him? This time he would not even have the support of Farel, who was settled in another city. Calvin could scarcely speak of his dilemma without bursting into tears. Yet he knew from the first that he could not resist the plea to return to Switzerland. He could not forget, or turn his back upon, the call that had come in Geneva when he had first gone as a stranger there.

If he had foreseen all that was to happen, he could hardly have been more wretched in his mind than he was already. There was good reason to fear the future. There would be disputes and abuse and shouting, as before; dogs set upon him in the street, guns fired under his window; outbursts of his uncontrollable anger followed by sleepless nights of repentance; sickness confining him to his bed, and endless duties calling him out when he was scarcely strong enough to stand; the death of his beloved wife.

It was to this that he was returning; and though he could not know as yet everything which would befall him, his heart was filled with fear. But another fear drove him on. What if Geneva were lost to the Reformation, through his weakness, through his cowardice? How then should he face his God? Would the blood of these souls not be upon his head?

Yes, yes—he must go back.

The Roman Catholic Church was rallying its forces. The Roman Catholic Church was striking back.

Where it still reigned supreme, it always had, of course, the power of fire and sword to crush its enemies. In Italy and Spain, for instance, Protestantism would not long threaten the rule of Rome. But the Roman Church had been challenged to reform itself. It was not enough merely to destroy opponents. Rome must put its house in order, and win the respect of men again.

It was a young Spanish nobleman named Ignatius Loyola who, more than any other single man, started his Church on the road to recovery. Loyola was a knight whose career as a soldier was ruined by the blast of a cannon ball. As he lay in bed, waiting for his wounds to heal, he began to read the lives of Christ and the saints, and he determined that henceforth his life should be more like theirs. When he was able to travel once again, he went to a monastery and took off his knightly armor, and then went out to beg his bread. For nearly a year he lived in a cavern, forcing himself to endure great suffering of body and of soul.

In this cavern he planned the self-discipline which later he wrote down in a book of *Spiritual Exercises*. Whoever would follow this way must meditate upon his own sins, and upon the punishment which he deserved. He must cultivate a sense of shame and sorrow; and in order to feel his sins the more keenly, he should go without light and warmth, and deprive himself of companionship and of unnecessary food. Then would come the call of Christ for volunteers in his holy warfare, and those who answered the call would yield themselves to a life of humiliation and self-sacrifice. There was a time for meditating upon the sufferings of Christ, and, to balance that, another time for thinking of the resurrection and the joys of the world to come. Such was the spiritual drill to which Loyola summoned all who shared his ideal of perfect service.

Loyola went to France, there to get the education that he lacked. In Paris he found companions to join him in his venture. Their plan was to journey to the Holy Land as missionaries, but the warfare raging at that time prevented them from obtaining passage. They determined, therefore, to put themselves at the service of the pope, who looked with favor upon this small but enthusiastic band of his followers. In 1540, they were given permission to organize themselves as the Society of Jesus, or "Jesuits." Loyola was elected head of the Society, and the numbers began to grow.

Absolute obedience was required of all who sought to become Jesuits. A member might be ordered to travel to a distant corner of the world as a missionary to savages; and he was expected to go without question or complaint. In time the Jesuits would win a reputation for unsurpassed heroism in all parts of the earth. They would also become known for their ruthless and relentless ways, for their belief that any method was justified so long as it served the Roman Church and the Society of Jesus. Meanwhile, the pope had found a powerful new organization—an army within his Church—to help throw back the forces of the Reformation.

The Jesuits, however, could not do everything. The whole Roman Church must act. It must have a Counter Reformation to offset the Protestant movement. In 1545, a council was called at Trent. Meeting off and on, whenever it was convenient, the council did not finish its work until 1563. But by that time it had remade the Roman Catholic Church into what it was to remain through the centuries to come.

Spurred on by the Jesuits, the Council of Trent rejected those beliefs upon which the Reformers took their stand. To Roman Catholics who leaned toward Protestant teachings, the council turned a deaf ear. It was declared that purgatory exists, and that indulgences have value. The traditions of the Church were said to have just as much authority as Scripture; and men were forbidden to interpret Scripture for themselves, since only the Church could truly understand the Bible. If anyone taught what was contrary to the decrees of the council, he was to be "anathema"—accursed! And this profession of faith was to be demanded of good Roman Catholics: "I acknowledge the holy catholic apostolic Roman Church as the mother and mistress of all churches, and I promise and swear true obedience to the Bishop of Rome as the successor of Saint Peter, Prince of the Apostles, and as the Vicar of Jesus Christ."

The door was shut firmly now upon the Reformation. The Roman Church was yielding nothing. But now, at least, everyone knew where the Roman Church stood. There could be no difference of opinion about doctrines, as before the Reformation, for the Council of Trent had defined the teachings of the Church, and the curse of Rome would fall upon all who ventured to differ.

The Church of Rome had closed its ranks, and become a solid army. From the pope and his cardinals, through bishops and priests, the orders would go forth; no one would dare to think for himself, much less disobey. To the ancient city of Rome, all the world that still professed the faith of that Church must turn and bow.

In 1564, a year after the Council of Trent had finished creating the new Church of Rome, John Calvin died. He too had built a kind of empire, and Geneva, the city of his labors, had become a school to which thousands went to learn the way of what was to be known as the Reformed, or sometimes the Presbyterian, Church.

Calvin did not, however, rule this empire as a prince, but rather as a teacher. Refugees driven by persecution from their native countries sat at his feet, hearing his sermons, absorbing his lectures. To those who could not come, his ideas went forth in the pages of his books, or in the endless stream of letters flowing from his pen. His teaching would one day bear fruit in Holland, in Scotland, even in France, where after fierce conflict and cruel suffering the Protestants would at last gain the right to live among their Roman Catholic neighbors.

There were many things to learn at Geneva. One was the manner of governing the Church: not through bishops, but, more democratically, through a consistory made up of ministers and laymen. It was a rigid enough rule, and there was no place in Geneva for anyone whom the Reformed Church leaders called a heretic. One such, Servetus by name, was even burned at the stake for his errors. Calvin would have preferred a more merciful death for him, but his wishes were brushed aside. Servetus, who was a heretic to Roman Catholics as well as to Reformers, would have fared no better elsewhere. Yet in Geneva it was not rule from above; the Church governed itself.

There was theology to learn at Geneva. Luther had never set his teaching all in order, and Melanchthon had made only a beginning at it. The clear mind of Calvin had gathered together in a system the doctrines of the Reformed Church, and his *Institutes* was a textbook for all to read.

But Calvin could not live forever, and not everyone would agree with all that he wrote in his books. His way of Church government might be changed, and Geneva might become just another city. Calvin was no pope, and Geneva did not claim to be another Rome.

The power that had gone out into the world was greater than Calvin or his writings. It was the power of the Word of God, set forth in the Bible and preached by the Church. The Church had learned to look to the Scriptures. What mattered from now on was not what the pope had said or what John Calvin said: it was what God had said, and what he was saying now.

If any man knew this, there was only one thing he would not dare to do. That was to disobey the commands that came, not from any earthly ruler, and not from Rome or from Geneva, but from the King of Kings.

CHAPTER 14

REFORMATION IN BRITAIN

THE books were dangerous, and a man had to be careful about letting it be known that he had read them. There was a secret room in London where one could go sometimes at midnight and talk about them into the small hours of the morning. There were barns and country houses where the readers of the books could gather, and feel that they were among friends. But it must be kept very quiet: no wind of the affair must get to the authorities. To read or to possess those books would be counted a crime in England.

The forbidden books were mostly Bibles, or portions of the Bible, translated into English. Along with them there were a few simple pamphlets, explaining the Lord's Prayer or the Ten Commandments. They had come down from the times of John Wycliffe; and the readers were descendants of Wycliffe's early followers, a century and more before. "Lollards," these folks were called, and to be a Lollard was to be a heretic. The government was not sure how many of them were left—not so many, it was hoped, since one of their most prominent leaders had been put to death. But there were still enough of them among the common people, leaderless now and looking for guidance mainly from their precious copies of the Bible. Though they seldom spoke of their opinions openly, they were opposed in several matters to the Church of Rome. They had no use for pilgrimages, or for lighting candles before the images of the saints. They did not believe that at the priest's words the bread and wine turned into the body and blood of Christ. They had got the mysterious name of "known men," perhaps because they claimed to know the Scriptures; but it was in their interests that they themselves should not be known.

The old literature that had come down from former days made their chief reading. But when Reformation ideas began to go abroad in Europe, there were new books to read. It was a dangerous business to import such writings across the English Channel; but there was profit in it for those who would take the risks, for the "known men" could be counted on to buy them when they could. And there were some who cared more about spreading the truth than about making money. Books that could not safely be sold were sometimes left at men's doors in the night, for them to find in the morning.

Among the common people, reading could be a dangerous adventure. At the Universities of Oxford and Cambridge, it was the business of scholars to read books. It would not matter there whether or not the Bible had been translated into English. Students could read the Latin version, against which there was no law; and later the Dutch scholar Erasmus gave them the New Testament in the Greek in which it had first been written. At Oxford, John Colet became so much in earnest about what the Bible really meant, and so critical of the abuses in the Church, that his enemies called him a heretic. But Colet died before the Reformation in Germany had much more than begun. It was the young men of Cambridge who led the way when times became more perilous for anyone who leaned to the new ideas; and before their generation was over, twenty-five of them died for their faith. Their crime was in believing the books they read, and especially the Scriptures, in opposition to the Roman Catholic Church.

Thomas Bilney was the first to walk the dreadful way to

peace of mind. The faith of the Reformation dawned upon him when the words of Paul struck home and shed a great light on all his struggle for holiness: "It is"—as the old version put it—"a true saying and worthy of all men to be embraced that Christ Jesus came into the world to save sinners, of whom I am the chief and principal." "O most sweet and comfortable sentence to my soul!" Bilney exclaimed. But to tell others that one was saved by faith in Christ's gospel and not by the fastings and penances and pilgrimages of the Roman Church—that was what was risky. Bilney was arrested, and after much argument he confessed, in part, that he had taught heresies which he ought not to teach again. He returned to Cambridge a free man, but full of grief within, fearing he had betrayed the truth. Nothing would console him—nothing but to go and preach again what he believed, and suffer the consequences. In August, 1581, he was burned at the stake. He had given to the poor, comforted prisoners and lepers, preached Christ's mercy. But he had not done enough until he had laid down his very life. Bilney was dead, but the gospel he and his Cambridge friends were preaching was not stilled.

Whether among "known men" in secret places or among scholars in the halls of learning, it was above all the Bible that was rousing men to life. Yet England had no English Bible except the copies of Wycliffe's translation that the authorities had not yet destroyed; and already Wycliffe's language was out of date and hard to understand. It was William Tyndale who resolved that Englishmen should have the Scriptures in words that all could read. "If God spare my life," he said to a scholar, "I will cause a boy that driveth the plough shall know more of the Scripture than thou dost."

But England was not the place in which to do the work; across the Channel it would be safer. Tyndale left his native country, never to return. From the Continent he sent back the New Testament, translated into English, and as much of the Old Testament as he lived long enough to put into the people's language. Also he sent some religious writings of his own, which showed how much he had learned from Martin Luther.

It was a perilous career he followed: even in Europe he was not out of reach of his foes. His good friend John Frith, who attacked the Roman Catholic teachings on the sacraments, went to a fiery death in England at the age of thirty. Tyndale too was marked for death; and by treachery he was delivered into the hands of the authorities who ruled the Netherlands.

Nothing could save him now. From the Holy Roman Empire, under whose power he had fallen, he could expect little mercy. The execution took place on an October day in 1536. He did escape the anguish of the flames, for before his body was burned at the stake the hangman strangled him. But before his breath was stopped, Tyndale summoned up the strength for a brief prayer: "Lord, open the king of England's eyes!" After that, the darkness fell on William Tyndale.

Darkness for him—but light for England! A year later, by the royal license of King Henry VIII, a Bible was published in the English tongue. In it was the work that Tyndale had completed. Now at last the Scriptures could go freely among the English people; and the humblest plowboy, as Tyndale had hoped, could read them for himself. Indeed, in 1538 the king gave orders that every person should be exhorted to read the Scriptures—"as that which is the very lively Word of God, that every Christian man is bound to embrace, believe and follow, if he look to be saved."

Tyndale was disgraced, sentenced, and strangled. But the Word of God, for which he died, was loose in the land.

King Henry VIII was never any friend to Tyndale. He had, in fact, once sent messengers to Europe to try to track him down and seize him. But Henry had had to change his mind about a number of things.

The king had once been a strong supporter of popes. He fancied himself a theologian; and when he heard of the heresies taught by Martin Luther, he took it upon himself to write a book against the German Reformer. It was absolutely necessary, Henry said then, that the whole Christian world should be united; and where would the Church be, he demanded, without the pope? For this he was rewarded with a title that he cherished dearly: "Defender of the Faith."

But that was before Henry wanted to get rid of his queen, Catherine of Aragon, with whom he had lived for eighteen years. The king grew doubtful—or so he said—as to whether he should ever have married her at all. For Catherine had once been married to Henry's brother Arthur, who later died. It was against the law of the Church for a man to marry his brother's widow, and that was what Henry had done. To be sure, the pope had given special permission for the wedding, and the king had not worried about it at the time. But now Henry raised the question, Did the pope have the right to allow such a marriage to take place? If not, then Henry had never really married at all. He was still a bachelor, free to take another wife. He knew who would make a more charming wife than Catherine—young Anne Boleyn. Perhaps she would give him the son he longed for so eagerly. Of all the children he and Catherine had had, only a girl named Mary was still living. But it was not of this hope, but of the matter of conscience, that he spoke when he argued that he should be free of his present queen.

The pope was not so ready to fall in with Henry's plans as the king had expected. For the pope was unwilling to admit that anyone who had sat in Saint Peter's chair had broken the law. Not knowing what else to do, he put off taking any action. Month after month of delay went by; and Henry, never a very patient man, decided to take matters into his own hands.

The "Defender of the Faith" called the bishops of England into assembly. He had decided that England, after all, did not require the services of the pope. Priests and bishops might object, but the English people would be unlikely to rally to their side. Long before this, the people of this island kingdom had felt resentment at paying tribute to a foreign ruler who lived in Rome.

To the bishops in assembly the order was issued: They were to announce that the king was "Supreme Head of the Church and Clergy in England." Afraid to refuse outright, the bishops had the courage to add that the king was head of the Church only "so far as the law of Christ allows." How much power "the law of Christ" allowed the king was open to debate.

It was no great victory for Henry. The pope neither gave in nor attacked the king. He continued to do nothing. Henry could wait no longer for a decision about his marriage. In January, 1533, he quietly married Anne Boleyn. By a stroke of fortune the old archbishop of Canterbury —head of the English bishops, and too strong even for Henry—had died the previous summer. There could be a new archbishop in his place; and Henry thought he could name the man who would serve him best.

Thomas Cranmer was a mild and cautious man. He was not ambitious; he wanted nothing less than to be archbishop. He was traveling in Europe when word came that the king wished him to take the highest post in the English Church, and it came as a most unwelcome surprise. He did not even feel free to accept the position. For, while staying in Germany, Cranmer had married the niece of a Protestant minister; and however Henry might feel about his own marriages, the king was not ready to accept the right of priests to take wives. Besides, it was plain that anyone who became archbishop would take his orders from Henry. Cranmer himself believed that the church should obey the king: but what kind of master would a monarch like Henry prove to be? However, one did not lightly refuse to accept the king's appointments. Henry was in a hurry, and Cranmer hastened home.

He was soon installed in Canterbury, having sworn at his consecration that, while he was loyal to the pope, he would never obey the pope in disobedience to the king. Soon afterward Cranmer carried out the purpose for which Henry had selected him. He announced, in the name of the Church, that Henry had never been married to Catherine of Aragon.

In 1534 the pope threatened to excommunicate the king. That same year, the Parliament of England passed the Act of Supremacy. The king, Parliament declared, was head of the English Church; and this time nothing was said about its being only "so far as the law of Christ allows." The king was given power to reform the Church however he saw fit. England had broken with Rome.

Henry was never sure, however, how far he wanted to go. He was glad enough to seize the monasteries, for this vast property enriched the royal treasury. Yet he was still determined to be the "Defender of the Faith." He clung to all he could of what the Roman Church had taught him. When, in 1547, Henry died, many wondered what to believe. And the old king, dying, wondered why there was so much strife and discontent in England. There was a cure for it, he said. The king who had had six wives, and beheaded two of them just as he slew every adviser who failed him or displeased him—this king declared that what England needed was more Christian love.

Six years later, in 1553, England was alight with bonfires to welcome a new sovereign. The boy king, Edward VI, who had followed Henry, was dead at the age of fifteen. Now the daughter of Catherine, who had kept her mother's Roman Catholic faith, was to be crowned Queen Mary.

Thomas Cranmer thought back over the six years that had passed since Henry's death. They had been good years for him. At his invitation, scholars and leaders from Europe had come to help him to plant the Reformation teachings in the heart of England. With King Edward friendly, they had enjoyed success. And their success had proved that the nation was ready for reform. Reformation had come none too soon. In one district, ten priests had been found who could not say the Lord's Prayer, and twenty-seven who did not know who composed it or where to find it! The common people who had so long hungered for Bible teaching had been getting their fill at last. The Cambridge scholars who had pioneered the new ideas, when the power of king and Church were set against them, were winning their reward.

Yet even under Edward the government had had to move carefully. There were many still whose loyalty to the old Church was not easily shaken. To keep what was good in the old, and not lose the truth of the new faith he had found—that was Cranmer's problem. Of all that he had done, perhaps he could be proudest of *The Book of Common Prayer*. From the service books of the past he took what seemed to him best; and then, with a touch of genius, he adapted the prayers and devotions of the Church through the ages, and produced a masterpiece. The beauty of the Anglican services he had written would be the glory of his Church's worship for centuries to come.

But now Mary was on the throne: and what did the future hold for Cranmer? The Protestant teachers were fleeing back to Europe, and many Englishmen were going with them. "If thou, O man of God," a bishop wrote to Cranmer, "do purpose to abide in this realm, prepare and arm thyself to die." Cranmer could not help knowing it was so, yet the archbishop, he thought, should remain at his post; and, true to his principles, he must submit to his new sovereign. Roman Catholic though she might be, the queen was head of the country— and, by act of Parliament, head of the Church!

Cranmer saw clearly what awaited him when, from his prison cell in Oxford, he watched Bishop Ridley and Bishop Latimer being burned at the stake. They went to their death cheerfully enough. "Play the man, Master Ridley," said Latimer; "we shall this day light such a candle, by God's grace, in England, as I trust shall never be put out." The gentle Cranmer himself had had a part in burning those opposed to him in happier days gone by. But was he prepared to suffer the same ordeal?

He must, he believed, willingly obey the queen; and so he could honestly say in public. But his foes were not content with that. He must, they demanded, also renounce the faith that he had taught. Almost alone among the three hundred martyrs who suffered under Mary, he lost his nerve. Worn down by his lengthy trial, he signed the document drawn up for him. He condemned the heresy of Luther, he declared that the pope was Christ's vicar on earth, he compared himself to Saul the persecutor and the thief on the cross. Yet still he must go to the stake.

One more chance to speak publicly remained to him. It was expected that he would repeat his confession of his faults. To the astonishment of his hearers, this is what they heard:

> And now I come to the great thing that so troubleth my conscience, more than any other thing that I said or did in my life: and that is my setting abroad of writings contrary to the truth, which here now I renounce and refuse as things written with my hand contrary to the truth which I thought in my heart, and written for fear of death.... And forasmuch as my hand offended in writing contrary to my heart it shall be first burned. And as for the Pope, I refuse him as Christ's enemy and Antichrist, with all his false doctrine. And as for the sacrament . . .

Shouts of fury interrupted him. "Stop his mouth! Take him away!"

Cranmer was led to the stake and bound there with a steel band. The flames leaped in the air; and Cranmer stretched out his right hand and held it in the fire until it was burned to nothing.

Cranmer had made his last great decision. And with the burning of the martyrs, England too made its decision. The rejoicing that had greeted Mary turned to hatred. She did not reign much longer. In 1558 she died, and the nation again was filled with gladness in welcoming another ruler— Queen Elizabeth.

Cautiously the new queen set about undoing the damage Mary had done. She abolished the Roman Mass in her private chapel. She declared herself, not "head," but "governor" of the Church in England. *The Book of Common Prayer* was brought back into use. Ministers were required to swear that they would submit to the supremacy of the queen. Thirty-nine Articles of faith were drawn up, to state what Anglicans believed, and with these doctrines the Reformers could not quarrel. Yet so far as she could keep old customs Elizabeth did so, not only because she herself loved them, but also to avoid offending too much those who clung at heart to the Roman Church.

Elizabeth was determined that all England should outwardly have the same faith. There would be no war of religion, as in Europe, to tear her kingdom in two. Above all, she was determined to defend herself and her country from the attacks of Roman Catholic nations across the English Channel.

One last attempt was made to overpower Elizabeth. Roman Catholic Spain sent a mighty fleet—the Spanish Armada—to invade England. On a famous July day of 1588 the fire that burned the Protestant martyrs was repaid. It was ships, however, that were burned. The great Armada fled in terror.

The nation was saved, and so was the Church of England. Roman Catholic foes abroad could not hope to try again. And woe betide any Roman priest who showed himself henceforth in England, while Elizabeth was queen!

For the sake of peace, the Church must be made to obey the ruler of the country: so the kings and queens of England thought. In the sister kingdom of Scotland, a young priest named John Knox came to a different view. Rulers, he taught, must be made to obey the gospel of Jesus Christ— even if it takes rebellion and bloodshed to compel them. He was no Thomas Cranmer, submitting for the sake of conscience to the ruling monarch. Knox's conscience would allow him to submit to nothing but what he believed to be God's truth. To her face he told the queen of Scotland: "When I preach I am not master of myself, but must obey Him who commands me to speak plain and to flatter no flesh upon the face of the earth."

It started for Knox on a cold January day in the year 1546 It was then that he heard George Wishart preach. Wishart was a preacher of the Reformed faith. He was not the first to call for Reformation in Scotland, nor the first to suffer for his views. Back in 1528, Patrick Hamilton, the first of the Scottish martyrs, was burned at the stake. But killing a man did not kill the hope of some reform—especially not in Scotland, where the Church had become a joke among the common people. Here was George Wishart, calling upon the nation to throw off the burden of the Roman Church and believe the gospel. And here was John Knox, like many another man, drinking in his words and preparing to walk in his steps.

Wishart was doomed. Cardinal Beaton, the most powerful man in Scotland, would not allow a preacher like this to live. Knox would gladly have gone with Wishart to his death, but the martyr would not let him. "Go back," he said, "one is sufficient for a sacrifice." Soon afterward Cardinal Beaton watched from St. Andrew's Castle in Edinburgh, while Wishart died in the flames to which he was condemned.

But Beaton himself had not much longer in this world. Three months later a party invaded St. Andrew's Castle. One of the intruders called upon the cardinal to repent; and then, declaring that he was "an obstinate enemy against Christ Jesus and his holy Gospel," ran a sword through his body.

Those who had dared to enter the castle stayed there, and prepared to defend themselves against a siege. To the castle Knox was invited; and there he was solemnly urged to take upon himself the work of preaching, if he hoped to escape God's wrath. The siege, however, could not last for long. Knox himself knew it, and was ready to take the consequences. Forces from France soon overpowered the defenders; and Knox, with the others, was arrested and sentenced to serve in the French galleys.

For nineteen months he was chained with other prisoners to his place in the ship, wearing out his strength upon the oars. A man stood over the victims with a whip, from time to time bringing it down upon the naked back of some prisoner whose

efforts were failing through exhaustion. Once the ship approached the shore of Scotland, and Knox could make out in the distance the tower of the castle where once he preached.

It was not, however, the cruelty of the galleys that filled Knox's soul with horror at the thought of the Roman Church. He had already made up his mind as to where he stood; and no cut of the lash could hurt him more than what he thought was the blasphemy of the Roman priest in saying Mass. For a man to stand at the altar, and claim some share in what Christ had done in pleading with God for sinful man—that is what Knox could not forgive. At the Communion table, no one could stand in Christ's place. Whatever the cost, this horrible idol, the Roman Catholic Mass, must go. And with that determination Knox bent to the oars—until such time as he should be free.

Freedom came at last for Knox, but never any long time of peace. Exiled again and again from Scotland, he made his way to Geneva. There, working side by side with John Calvin, he might have found happiness, but he could not forget his native land. What he learned in Geneva was to be used at home. If he ever had his way, Scotland would accept the faith of the Presbyterian Church.

His chance came at last. The nobles of Scotland were rallying to Knox's side. In 1560 the Church was organized along the lines that Knox approved. Each congregation would rule itself, and choose its own ministers; and it was provided that ministers must be well educated and fit to carry out their office. Superintendents were to take the place of bishops. The congregations would establish schools, so that all the people would receive an education. Not until after Knox's death was the presbytery set up to govern the churches in a district. Later, the leaders hoped that the congregations, through their elders, would rule not only in religion but in all the affairs of life in town, village, and countryside. Thus the Church would once more rule the country—not through a pope and bishops, but according to the system that had been learned from Calvin at Geneva.

The lords of Scotland were on Knox's side, but the queen was not. Beautiful, quick-witted, full of energy, Mary Queen of Scots was a firm Roman Catholic. She could have no hope at the time of bringing back the Roman Catholic faith to Scotland; but she could, and she did, have her private Masses said by priests in her chapel, while she waited for a better opportunity to win her battle against her people. At the thought of Mass being said in the city where he was preaching, Knox's indignation knew no bounds. Queen she might be, but Knox never wearied of attacking her religion—whether in the pulpit or to her very face. At last she was forced to resign her throne, and Knox could not forgive his country that the Roman Catholic queen was allowed to flee to England. A great plague from God's own hand would fall on Scotland, Knox declared, if she were permitted to escape. And he was not altogether wrong: for while she lived, the peace of Scotland was in danger, and Mary Queen of Scots was at length beheaded on the charge of conspiring against Queen Elizabeth's life.

Death came for Knox in 1572 and he was not sorry. He was exhausted by his long struggle for the faith by which he lived. He would gladly have died much sooner. "Lord," he wrote in 1565 "in thy hands I commend my spirit; for the terrible roaring of guns and the noise of armour do so pierce my heart that my soul thirsteth to depart." For Knox there was never any quiet. But the Church that survived him was strong of spirit, ready to resist to the death every attack upon its faith. The Church of Scotland was built to be a fighting Church.

In 1603 the long reign of Queen Elizabeth came to a close. James VI of Scotland, the son of Mary Queen of Scots, became James I of England, and at last the two kingdoms were united. James was no Roman Catholic. He was ready to accept the Anglican Church, and to be its firmest supporter. He was all the more ready to be an Anglican, because he knew how hard it was for rulers to bend the Church of Scotland to their will. Life for him so far had been a constant struggle with Presbyterian ministers. A Scottish presbytery, he said, "agrees with monarchy as well as God and the devil." Bishops, he hoped, would be more obedient servants. "No bishop, no king," was his favorite saying.

A Church that rebuked kings was a Church to be feared and hated. For it was a Church that had no fears, except the fear of God.

CHAPTER 15

TO THE NEW WORLD

KING James was annoyed He had been plagued by Pres byterians in Scotland; and now, in England, must he put up with Puritans?

The king was glad to take the Church of England just as he found it. A great many of his subjects, however, were not so easily pleased. They did not object to the nickname "Puritan," for what they stood for was a pure Church, and in their opinion the Anglican Church had no right to be called pure. It was, they said, still too much like the Church of Rome. The Reformation had not gone far enough.

The trouble had started in Elizabeth's reign; she, like James, had had little patience with troublemakers. She was determined that the Anglican services should be as attractive as possible to those who loved the beauty and the glamour and the mystery of the old Roman Catholic worship. Ministers, she decided, must wear the caps and white linen surplices designed for them; whatever they might think of it, they must read everything set down in front of them in *The Book of Common Prayer*. There were to be no exceptions. In vain did her own bishops try to discourage the queen from forcing her ceremonies upon the Church. In vain did Puritans protest that the New Testament never taught Christians to worship in this way, and that the Anglican services made ministers look like Roman Catholic priests. Elizabeth would not be disobeyed.

That was the beginning of the trouble, but far from the end of it. There was little disagreement as to what the Church should believe and teach: the Church of England followed the teachings of John Calvin closely enough to satisfy the Puritans. What worried the Puritan party was the way the Church was organized and ruled. Would the New Testament, they began to ask, approve of bishops? And if government by bishops was not right, what should be put in its place?

Here the Puritans could not agree among themselves. Some said that a Presbyterian Church was the only kind that Scripture would allow. Others had a different answer. Each congregation, they maintained, ought to be independent of all others; it ought to rule itself, and into its membership no person who was not plainly leading a Christian life should be admitted. Those who favored such a Church as this got the name of Independents, or Congregationalists. Some of them went so far as to break off from the Church of England and form little congregations of their own. On one point, however, everybody thought alike—bishops, and Presbyterians, and Independents. Everybody thought that there was no room in England for any kind of Church except the one in which he himself believed.

With the Puritans, King James had no sympathy whatsoever. Who were these men who ventured to criticize a Church that had been established by the authority of royal law? James had two great convictions. One was that kings were sacred, and entitled to unquestioning obedience. The other was that his Maker had given him a great mind, with special talents for understanding theology. If the Puritans would not bow to the monarch's will without dispute, then James felt equal to the task of getting the better of them in argument. At Hampton Court, in 1604, he met with their leaders. On the king's side were several bishops and other officials of the Church of England, but it was mainly James who did the talking. On one point only did he consent to the demands of the Puritans: he was willing to have a new translation of the Scriptures made. From this decision resulted what to this day is called the King James version of the Bible.

On nothing else, however, would the king yield. The ceremonies of the Church of England were going to stay. He was satisfied that he had given a good account of himself in the dispute. "If this is all your party has to say," he exclaimed in contempt, "I will make them submit, or I will drive them out of this land—or else worse!"

The Hampton Court conference broke up, and the king had no doubt that he had put the Puritans in their place.

It was shortly after this that a little group of people began to meet for worship in the village of Scrooby, in the north of England. They were mostly farmers and craftsmen from the countryside and neighboring hamlets. They were intelligent folk, but few were educated or could claim any high station in life. They had come together because they were opposed to bishops, and to the forms and ceremonies of the Church of England. They had decided to set up their own congregation and worship in their own way.

If the king was set on driving such as these out of the land, this congregation was willing to be driven. It was not that they were suffering much persecution: they were scarcely thought worthy of attention. They had their own reasons for leaving England. They could not bear to mingle with their sinful neighbors, or remain in the same country with the Anglican Church. In 1608 they moved to Holland, going first to Amsterdam and then to Leyden, where again they formed their own congregation under the leadership of John Robinson, their pastor.

But Holland proved to have its drawbacks too. There was always the danger that the Spaniards, who formerly ruled Holland, would return and subject them to the horrors of the Spanish Inquisition. But even if that did not happen, the fact remained that their children were growing up in a foreign city, out of touch with the land of their fathers, forgetting even their native language. Moreover, Holland did not, in their opinion, set a good example of Christian living; their children might too easily be tempted into evil ways. Some of the young people ran away from home to become soldiers or to go to sea. The congregation saw nothing to be gained by returning to England. Where, then, should they go?

Across immense sea miles lay the new continent of America. Might they hope there to plant the gospel in the far places of the earth? Would there not be room in that vast territory to found the kind of Church and community in which they believed? It was a daring thought, full of unknown terrors. The water that must be crossed was deep and wide, and many had already perished in it. Savages would be awaiting them on the shore. Yet settlers from England had already braved the dangers and set up habitations in Virginia. These pioneers would not be the first to go.

Even so, the number of those who finally determined to leave Leyden was small. The little party journeyed first to England, where it was joined by another group of like-minded people. In September of 1620, a company of about a hundred souls set sail from Plymouth in a ship called the *Mayflower*. In November the rocky shore of New England was sighted, and a month later the first house was erected in the Plymouth of the New World. The Pilgrim Fathers had arrived.

During the first winter, disease struck the little settlement whose members had been weakened by the hardships of the long sea voyage. About half their number died. Others came, however, to take their place. The pioneers had a Church that was to their liking, for it was all their own, a law to itself, a congregation separated from the wicked world left behind across the sea.

Ten years later America called to another group of Englishmen and their families who were willing to risk the perils of the ocean and an unknown land. These new pioneers had never been so rash as the first Pilgrims. They had been careful not to separate themselves from the Church of England; yet in that Church they could not find happiness or peace. They too saw the hope of a new community where the Church would be as they—and no one else—decided. There were men of means and men of education in their number. There were men of imagination too, resourceful men who foresaw that if only they could get established across the ocean, they would be beyond the reach of any Parliament or king. They did not speak of that to the authorities. The first step was simply to organize a trading company, like others that had been formed, with a charter granting them the right to settle in New England. The next step was to take the charter and move to America. The rest would take care of itself.

In 1630, a large party gathered at Southampton to sail from England. John Cotton, a distinguished Puritan minister who would later join them on the other side of the sea, preached a farewell sermon. His text for the occasion summed up the spirit of the great adventure. He took it from II Samuel 7:10:

> Moreover I will appoint a place for my people Israel, and will plant them, that they may dwell in a place of their own, and move no more; neither shall the children of wickedness afflict them any more, as beforetime.

Two months later, on a clear June day, the ship was in the Gulf of Maine. John Winthrop, leader of the expedition, wrote in his journal that they were greeted by "so pleasant a sweet air as did much refresh us, and there came a smell off the shore like the smell of a garden."

They had come to "a place of their own."

The new arrivals settled in Massachusetts Bay, spreading out to form towns at Salem, Charlestown, Boston, Roxbury, and Dorchester. They had come too late to plant crops for that year, and a hungry winter followed. The settlers were forced to live on hardtack left over from the voyage and the smelts and clams with which the ocean supplied them. Many lived in bark wigwams or tents made of sailcloth. It was not an inviting prospect for others left in England, and only a few hundred persons joined the colony in the next two years. In 1633 however, the numbers began to grow, for in that year William Laud became archbishop of Canterbury.

England had a new king by this time—Charles I. James had had his theories about the divine right of kings; Charles was doubly determined to put them into practice. The king must rule, and no law and no Parliament would restrain him. To make matters worse, his wife was a Roman Catholic. Like his father, Charles believed that bishops would be the mainstay of the throne. In William Laud he found an archbishop who would be only too willing to stamp out the Puritan party in England.

Under Laud, the ceremonies of the Church of England were going to be enforced—not only the older ones, but new ceremonies that he himself brought in. There was to be one form of worship in England, and one only. He would decide what it was to be. Failure to obey his orders would bring severe and certain punishment. He even insisted strictly that the "Book of Sports"—a declaration of years before, advising Christians to engage in games and recreation after the Sunday service—should be read from the pulpit. It went hard with Puritan ministers who, being opposed to Sunday games, defied the archbishop's command. Angry attacks upon the bishops burst into print, and the authors of them, when they could be found, suffered cruel penalties. Scotland suffered too. Not understanding the feelings of the Scottish people, Charles decreed that a new liturgy should be used in the Church of Scotland. In opposition, Scotsmen allied themselves under a "National League and Covenant" to defend the Presbyterian Church.

Even the hardships of New England looked attractive now, compared to the persecution of Puritans in England. Within ten years after Laud became archbishop, twenty towns and churches had been founded in Massachusetts Bay, and sixteen thousand people had sought refuge there.

The rule of Charles and Laud could not go on. The Parliament of England, spurred on by Puritan leaders, rose in opposition. The people of New England heard interesting news from across the sea. In the old land Laud had been beheaded. Parliament called together the Westminster Assembly to draw up a new statement of faith, from which came the Westminster Confession and the Larger and Shorter Catechisms of the Presbyterian Church. It was even planned to force the Presbyterian system upon England, but the plan was never carried out. The news grew more interesting still: King Charles himself had been put on trial, convicted of treason against his own country, and sentenced to death. When the king had been beheaded, Oliver Cromwell became "protector" of England in place of a king. The government of the Church by bishops was ended for the time, and all types of Puritan churches were at liberty to go their own way under Cromwell. The great reform of the Church, for the sake of which so many Puritans had fled to America, seemed to have arrived.

The good news from England drew some of the Massachusetts settlers back to their native land—some, but not many. For it was now not England, but Massachusetts Bay, which was their home. They had looked for liberty here, and they had found it. Things had worked out very much as they had planned. The "trading company" that had originally been founded had turned into a colony that ruled itself—still under the control of Parliament in theory, but really free and independent because it was so far away. Why go back to England where the future was so uncertain? And when the revolution in England was all over, and another king who persecuted Puritans was back on the throne, the New England settlers could congratulate themselves on their wisdom in staying where they were safe.

The settlers in Massachusetts Bay had found liberty. But it was liberty only for themselves, not for others. The first leaders could not keep their power forever. But before they gave it up, they made sure that in their colony only church members should be allowed to vote. To be a church member in Massachusetts was a very different thing from belonging to the Church of England. In the old country all were baptized into the Church and all were members except the few who were cast out. In Massachusetts, the church could pick and choose those who were thought fit for membership. Whoever failed to get admission into the church would have no vote in the town. No difference was made between rich and poor. A rich man might be frowned upon by the church of his town; a poor man could have all the rights of a citizen which the rich man could not buy or gain in any other way except by proving himself fit to be called a Christian.

In 1631, there arrived in Massachusetts a young English minister named Roger Williams. He was soon in trouble. Nothing was more useful to the settlers there than the charter by which they held their lands, and now this young outsider began to teach that the king had never had the right to grant the charter. The land belonged, not to the king, but to the Indians. Moreover, he declared that no government had the right to punish men for matters of worship and conscience: government was only for the purpose of keeping the peace and preventing crime. To the Puritans of Massachusetts, there was no worse crime and no greater danger to the peace than false religion. But they could not say that Roger Williams was unconcerned about religion. For he began his stay in Boston by calling the church in that town "impure"—so impure that he could not bring himself to join it. Its members had belonged to the Church of England, and it was time that they confessed their sin in not having separated from the Anglican Church long

before they sailed for America. Salem, he thought, was better than Boston, but even there he continued to attack the Puritans of Massachusetts Bay.

The older settlers were not slow to take offense at this aggressive newcomer, and Williams was not long left in peace. In 1635, he was banished from Salem, and it was planned to put him aboard a ship for England. Learning of the plot, he lost no time in making his escape. In the cold New England winter he fled across the country, finding refuge with an Indian friend. Finally he reached the head of Narragansett Bay, and, in token of what he called "God's merciful providence to him in his distress," the name of Providence was given to the settlement he founded there. He purchased the land from the Indians, believing that to them belonged the right to dispose of the country they so long had owned. Thus came into being the colony of Rhode Island.

Williams had been thinking further about religion. Already in England there had sprung up congregations of Baptists, who maintained that children ought not to be baptized until they reached an age when they could answer for their own faith. Williams was now convinced that they were right; and in Providence, when he and less than a dozen others were baptized, the first Baptist Church in America was formed.

Rhode Island was different from the other settlements. Elsewhere there was one church, and one alone. Men did not dream that two or more kinds of churches could live together in the same country. But Williams dreamed it, and in Rhode Island persecution was unknown. All might worship as they chose. A man's faith was for his own conscience, not for the government, to decide.

For the first time there was a place with liberty for men of all beliefs. Rhode Island was small, but all who wished might come to it and no questions would be asked about religion.

America, as a whole, was large; and if other colonies were not yet ready to follow the example of Providence, still there was room for everyone who longed for shelter from the wars and tumults and persecutions of Europe. In Maryland already there was a resting place for Roman Catholics. Soon in Pennsylvania, Quakers, who had been whipped in England and Massachusetts Bay, could find a refuge.

In the New World there was a place for everyone to go. In the New World there was space—vast, immense, beyond all imagination—and in that space was freedom.

$\mathcal{P}art\ IV$

THE WORLD SHAKES
THE CHURCH

CHAPTER 16

CHANGING TIMES

THE great spaces of America were calling. The invitation rang in eager ears—not in England only, but in Scotland, in Ireland, in Switzerland, in Germany. "Come over to America—come over and be free!"

In many a town and village of the Old World the talk was of the land of opportunity that lay across the sea. one man might hold in his hand a leaflet sent by someone in America— someone who knew how badly servants and laborers and craftsmen and farmers were needed, if a nation was to grow and money was to be made in the American colonies. The man with the leaflet could paint a rosy picture for his friends.

"Do you see what it says? No taxes, high wages, cheap food! What more could you ask?"

"Yes," another might object, "but where would I get the money to pay my way across?"

"No problem in that," the first would answer. "Hire yourself out as a servant for a year or two when you get there. You'll not only earn your passage but save enough to buy a piece of land. There is plenty of land in America. You can have it almost for the asking. After that you will be independent.

Were you ever independent here?"

No, they had not known what it was like in Europe to have more than enough food to eat and money in their pockets. The poor could scarcely feed their families, let alone improve their lot in life. Even those who could raise a little capital could see no future in countries ruined by war and wasted by bad government. America sounded like the place of dreams-come-true. A century after the Pilgrim Fathers had set foot on Plymouth Rock settlers by the thousands were pouring into the New World.

Unfortunately the picture had been painted brighter than it was. Many of the hopeful families who set out to find happiness in America never got there; in the crowded, filthy ships, little better than those used to transport Negro slaves from Africa, disease claimed countless lives. Those who survived the passage did not find the freedom they had expected awaiting them on the shore. For the strong and the ruthless found ways to take advantage of the weak and ignorant; immigrants who had believed that they had money enough to begin a new life discovered that the costs of the journey had mysteriously increased, and they could not even pay their way. Thousands were forced to sell themselves into a kind of slavery for years to come, working for nothing to meet their debts. And when at last they gained their liberty, the cheap land they had dreamed of turned out to be wilderness country, where only endless labor and hardship could win a living from the soil.

Yet still they came, and if many perished, others survived, and won their freedom, and planted their little farms along the frontier. It was not for freedom to worship that they had come, but for freedom to live more happily than in the Old World they had left behind. It was not to escape religious persecution that these newer settlers risked the perils of sea and wilderness, but to escape the bitter, crushing poverty they had known from birth.

To great numbers of them, the Church meant little. In the old lands from which they had come, each country had its own national Church; and the people were born and baptized and brought up in it, and almost everyone was a member. They took it as a matter of course, like the language that they spoke or the scenery amidst which they lived. But although all belonged to the Church in theory, in practice few cared about it It was not their affair. The government and the ministers were responsible for the Church—not the common people.

In America everything was different The settlers did not automatically become members of a national Church. Entering the country was not the same thing as entering a congregation. Many of the congregations m the New World had been founded by religious folk who wished, not to bring everybody into the Church, but to keep out the halfhearted and the unworthy. If, in this new land, people wanted to stay away from the Church, nothing was easier; the difficulty might be in getting in. Moreover, on the frontier the settlers were often well out of reach of any congregation or minister. They could live their lives almost as if no Church existed.

Soon there were more persons outside the Church than in it. If all these souls were to be won to Christ, it was time for the ministers and others who cared to bestir themselves. The problem did not greatly trouble the older settlements like Boston. Whatever life might be like on the farther frontiers, it seemed respectable enough in the communities, now nearly a century old, along the New England coast.

There were, however, German settlers in Pennsylvania who were less content. True Christian faith, they thought, was dying. They had seen it happening in Germany, before they ever came to America. Like other Germans who shared their views, they got the name of pietists. The Church, they complained, had settled down and ceased to grow. The Church was satisfied if men merely believed what they were taught. Religion, the pietists declared, is more than what a man believes with his head: it is how he feels m his heart, how he prays, how he lives. True religion is an experience, which needs the inspiration of constant Bible-reading and must then reach out to touch the lives of others. So these pietists had believed when they had lived in Germany; and on coming into the New World, they had brought their earnestness along. Already they had stirred up a new religious life among their own people in Pennsylvania.

In New Jersey, a young Dutch Reformed pastor began to denounce the religion that was satisfied with an outward show of faith: each soul, he declared, must be converted. The movement that he started spread among the Presbyterians of Pennsylvania. Later, in Virginia, Baptist farmers became preachers, visiting the mountain settlements and calling upon the people to repent.

In the little town of Northampton, Massachusetts, a young man named Jonathan Edwards was at this time pastor of the Congregational Church. In America there was no more brilliant mind than his; and his deep thoughts about the majesty and the power and the beauty of God would one day be written down in books that would make him famous. Meantime he was already winning fame because of the sermons he was preaching in this town of two hundred families. It was not just the sermons themselves that were being talked about: it was what they did to those who heard them.

The young preacher never wearied of bringing his people face to face with their sins. He spared nobody: there was a warning for all.

"Look over your past life," he would urge his congregation. "How little regard you have had to the Scriptures, to the Word preached, to Sabbaths and sacraments! What revenge and malice have you been guilty of toward your neighbors! How much of a spirit of pride has appeared in you! What low thoughts you have had of God and what high thoughts of yourselves!"

Some were angry, but others were troubled. To be rid of their burden of guilt, they made their way to the minister's door to seek his advice. Religion became the talk of everyone. In six months, Edwards said later, over three hundred souls were "savingly brought home to Christ." News of what was happening spread to neighboring communities, throughout New England, then across the sea to England and Scotland.

No two people were alike, and each had his own problems. Yet the way of conversion, as Jonathan Edwards himself described it, was in most cases very much the same. First a person was overpowered by a sense of guilt; he felt himself beyond any hope or help. He knew that he deserved nothing but punishment from God. Then came the peace of knowing that God would take away his sins, if he would but put his trust in Christ. Life became changed, and a new man was born: now everything became "beautiful, and sweet, and pleasant," and everywhere he saw the glory of God.

The excitement of these conversions rose to feverish heights in 1740, when a great English preacher named George Whitefield visited America. His amazing voice— which a crowd of 20,000 could clearly hear—rang through the colonies along the Atlantic shore. A mighty wave of feeling ran through America—the Great Awakening had arrived.

High were the hopes of Jonathan Edwards, and of many others like him. "The new Jerusalem," it was said, was coming down from heaven. The poor would feel the effects of the gospel, even the Indians would be won to a Christian and civilized way of life, and the Kingdom of God would begin to appear in America.

If some rejoiced, however, others grew bitter. The evangelists who had aroused so many souls could not control the feelings they had awakened. Many people were swept away in a great outburst of frenzy—only to sink into old ways again when the excitement was over. The opponents of the Great Awakening said that no good would come from this religious madness. Jonathan Edwards himself was driven from his Northampton pulpit, because he set such a strict rule upon the conduct of members of his church.

Yet a way had been found to reach the people of the frontiers. In the land of the free, it seemed, men and women must be won to Christ by making them want to come. Not having been brought up in the Church, they must be converted. The day of the religious revival had come in America.

In 1738 a priest of the Church of England, John Wesley, returned from a visit to America. It was two years since he had made the westward voyage: but the music he had heard on shipboard still resounded in his memory. He had not been listening for music; he had been wondering if he was about to die. The wind was whipping the sea against the ship, and it seemed as though the boat were surely doomed. Many of the English passengers aboard were screaming, and Wesley was ashamed to find that even he was afraid of death. Then, above the roaring of the gale and the crying of the frightened passengers, he heard singing. Twenty-six Germans, members of the Moravian Church, were singing hymns. Theirs was a long tradition of faithfulness and courage. The Moravian Church had first arisen among some of the followers of John Hus; and through centuries of difficulty the fellowship had remained alive. In recent years they had found a friend in Count Zinzendorf of Saxony, who hoped to see a warmer "religion of the heart" spring up within Christian men. He was glad to give refuge on his estate to the persecuted Moravians; and there they built a town named Herrnhut. Now a company of them were on their way to America—once more in peril, and, as ever, singing.

Wesley, the fervent and scholarly clergyman of the Church of England, was anxious for his life. And a little group of poor and simple folk from Germany were fearlessly pouring out their hearts in songs of faith and praise!

That had been two years ago. Now Wesley was home again. He had gone to America in order to preach to the Indians of Georgia. As he looked back, he was unhappy about his visit. "I," he wrote, "who went to America to convert others, was never myself converted to God." All his life he had been seeking holiness. His mother had taught him as a child to be systematic in his search for God. She herself, while caring for her nineteen children, had always set aside two hours each day for meditation. As a tutor at Oxford, John Wesley had been the leader of a small group of young men who were trying to become more Christian. It was called the Holy Club. The members set themselves strict rules to follow: they must pray at regular times, partake of Holy Communion frequently meet to read together and discuss religion. They made it their practice also to visit poorhouses and prisons, to bring comfort where they could; and all the money they could spare was given to charity. There were not many of them, and they were laughed at throughout Oxford University. Because their lives were so methodical, they soon were nicknamed "Methodists" in scorn.

But Wesley was not satisfied. He had never been satisfied with himself; and in the Moravian Germans he had met on shipboard and in America he found men who were, he was convinced, more Christian than he. Back in England, he sought out the Moravians in London. On the evening of May 24, 1738, he sat in a hall in Aldersgate Street where a religious meeting was being held, and listened while someone read from a book by Luther. The reader came to the place where Luther wrote of what faith does for men—and all at once Wesley understood it. The meaning of the gospel came alive to him. "I felt my heart strangely warmed," he said. "I felt I did trust in Christ, Christ alone, for salvation; and an assurance was given me that he had taken away *my* sins, even *mine*, and saved me from the law of sin and death."

Wesley had found the peace he had been looking for. He had felt the gospel in his own soul. To strengthen himself in his new conviction, he traveled to Germany and lived for a time among the Moravians at Herrnhut. Now he was ready to begin his preaching in his native country.

But where was he to preach? To the bishops and most of the ministers of the Church of England, Wesley's Methodist movement seemed like madness. There was a fire in this preaching of which they were afraid. Strange events took place when Methodist preachers mounted the pulpit. Dozens of people fell to the ground, screaming, weeping, jerking as though in a convulsive fit. Scenes like these were far from the dignity of *The Book of Common Prayer*; and the authorities of the Church of England doubted whether the good done by the revival was equal to the harm. Pulpit after pulpit was closed to John Wesley. Flaming with the desire to preach and win new converts, he found himself shut out of the churches. Where could he go?

It was George Whitefield, who had been one of the young men at Oxford with Wesley in earlier days, who solved the problem. Whitefield was back from America. There he had preached to Indians—savages. But there were savages in England too. What about the rough and ignorant miners of Bristol? What about the masses of poor and wretched people who had moved into factory towns—for whom the Church of England was doing nothing? Whitefield had preached in jails. If no one would give him a pulpit from which to proclaim his gospel, why should he not go to the mine heads and preach out of doors?

John Wesley was not so sure. He loved the Church of England, with its order and its beauty. He had been no less than a dignified tutor at Oxford University. Surely it would be out of place for him to become a preacher to crowds gathered by chance at a street corner. Yet it was either open-air preaching, or none at all. Besides, Whitefield was making a success of it. Some of his hearers might curse, but others wept; and it rejoiced his heart to see the tears making a path down the grimy cheek of a hardened miner. Wesley was at last persuaded to follow the example of his fellow Methodist.

Once started, he never ceased his preaching to the crowds of poor and ignorant that gathered where he went. They did not always come in a mood to hear the gospel. Stones were thrown at Wesley. Once he was seized by the hair and dragged into the midst of a furious mob; yet he did not stop his sermon. "Knock his brains out—kill him at once!" yelled the crowd. Wesley began to pray, and the man who had begun the riot turned and said, "Sir, I will spend my life for you: follow me, and not a soul here shall touch a hair of your head."

By foot and on horseback he traveled 250,000 miles, and preached over 50,000 sermons. Methodist societies were organized all over England, for prayer and discussion of the Christian life, and in these the new converts to Christianity never wearied of telling of their experiences. What they could not express in their own words they sang—in the 6,500 hymns written by John Wesley's brother Charles. Such music of faith and praise as John Wesley had heard on shipboard years before now rang through England.

Wesley would, however, have been sad to know what happened in the very year he died. To the end, which came to him in 1791, he never thought of himself as anything other than a minister of the Church of England. His Methodist societies were meant only to help the Church, to stir up new life where religion was dead or dying. Yet in the Church of England there turned out to be no place for Wesley's movement. Once he had been laid to rest, the Methodists separated from the Anglican Church and established a new Church of their own.

The Holy Club of Oxford had become a Church which would spread across the sea—to America, to Canada, to Africa, to Australia—and count its members in the millions.

The revival preaching had turned thousands to the Church in America and Britain. But there were thousands of others who were turning away. For many had begun to think that Christianity was very superstitious, and unworthy to be believed by an educated man.

What need, they argued, is there for God to reveal himself in Christ? We can discover all we need to know by using human reason and common sense! There is, no doubt, some kind of God. Some power must have made the universe and set it going. But only the ignorant, they said, would believe that God ever interferes with the world or breaks the eternal rules that he has made. Miracles, it would seem, were impossible and absurd. No enlightened person would listen to such tales— stories invented in ancient times, before mankind had learned to think reasonably about life.

The age of doubt had begun. And besides doubt, there was in many hearts a great bitterness toward the Church. The pietists and the Methodists were trying to help the poor—but had not the Church usually been on the side of the rich and the strong?

In France the bitterness in men's hearts turned into revolt against the age-old evils of the land. Rebels rose up and overthrew the government and beheaded the king and queen. They stripped the Church of its power. Priests were drowned, nuns were whipped; and so little had the Christian faith meant to the common people, who had long ago become Christian only because they were forced to, that there were few to rise to the defense of the Church. The storm blew over, and the revolution came to an end, but the Church in France was never so strong again.

The Church had begun to meet opposition. In Britain and America it was still respectable to be Christian: even educated men could call themselves Christian, without, however, believing all that the Church had taught in the unenlightened centuries behind. Those who were not swayed by the revival movements preferred to show their Christianity in good deeds alone: the faith that their fathers had held seemed to be a thing of the past.

It was liberty that men were looking for. Once the colonists had crossed an ocean for the sake of liberty of worship. Now their children, and the new arrivals in the New World, were interested in other kinds of freedom. Freedom to govern themselves was what the citizens of America most wanted now. In 1776 the American colonies broke away from the Old World: the colonies would form a nation of their own.

There were Anglicans in America, and Presbyterians, and Roman Catholics. There were Quakers and Congregationalists, Baptists and Methodists and Lutherans and Moravians— every kind of religious faith had been planted somewhere, it seemed, in the vast New World. There were men with no religion at all, or the "reasonable" religion they had worked out for themselves.

This was to be the land of freedom. And in this freedom there would be liberty to worship as a man might choose, or not to worship at all. The Constitution of the United States of America declared that Congress should make no law to establish any religion, or to prevent anyone from practicing the religion in which he believed.

Freedom—freedom for faith at last! And freedom to worship meant also freedom to doubt. The Churches would all be free; and the people would be free also to scorn the Churches.

The Christian Church must stand on its own feet now. The Church must win its way, and prove itself—or perish.

CHAPTER 17

DANGEROUS FRONTIERS

THE Church was like a stream that had divided into countless brooks and rivers, flowing in all directions. Instead of "the Church" there were now "the Churches": one in Christ, but each going under a name of its own, and doing its work as seemed wisest and best.

It was not enough for the Churches to hold their own. They had to exert themselves to keep up with the times. For mankind was pushing forward. In the 1800's there were always new trails to break, new frontiers to cross.

In America there was, to begin with, the physical frontier— hills and streams, uncleared forests, desert and mountains. Settlers were penetrating ever deeper into the continent. Wherever they went, the Churches must follow, for if there was any place, more than another, where the gospel was needed it was on the frontier. The new communities were being forged by hardy men, and the life was rough and rowdy. They cursed and swore; they filled themselves with homemade whisky. Sunday was just another day in the week. Far from a police force, a man's property, and even his life, was not always safe any more.

The Churches had already found a way to reach the pioneers: through a religious revival. It was worth trying again. Why not hold the meetings out of doors, and plan for several days of preaching? All that was needed was a hollow square, with hewn logs for seats. Anxious enough for a change from the routine of daily life, the people were glad to come. Some might come only to get drunk—but at least the camp meeting offered a holiday! From as far as a hundred miles away, the people thronged to the revivals. Some slept in their wagons; others built shelters out of branches. It was a time for noise and confusion. A dozen different hymns might be sung at once by the thousands gathered at the meeting. They loved to shout:

> This day my soul has caught on fire,
>> *Hallelujah!*
> I feel that heaven is coming nigher,
>> *O glory Hallelujah!*

Sometimes a whole community was transformed by the revival. But sometimes, too, ministers and church members were dismayed by the wild commotion, so that they declared it was a better revival when there was quietness and dignity. Meantime, the Churches on the frontier went about their work, keeping a strict watch over their members. All must submit to discipline for such sins as drunkenness and gambling and wife-beating and stealing and dishonest business deals; and the punishment was that they were denied the Communion or were put out of the Church. Colleges began to spring up: for the revivals led many young men to dedicate themselves to the ministry, and where there was no other means of education the Churches had to provide places where ministers could be trained. The Presbyterians preferred to send educated men to the frontier. The Baptists and the Disciples of Christ made use of zealous farmers, even when they were not educated, to preach to others. The Methodists met the problems of the great distances by appointing circuit riders—ministers to travel over wide areas, sometimes covering several hundred miles and preaching to twenty or thirty communities.

Still men pushed westward. Gold and silver drew them into the farther west, even to the Pacific coast. The great plains attracted cattlemen, and cowboys began to man the ranges. With the building of railroads to span the distances, the spaces filled up with homesteaders. The Churches followed the railroads. The steam engines that took new settlers into the heart of America could equally well carry the ministers of Christ; and all the denominations were busy organizing congregations in the towns and farming centers that grew along the railway lines. The Young Men's Christian Association, first formed in England, played its part, holding services at stations of the Union Pacific for people going west, even for the track layers taking the steel ribbons farther across the continent.

The Churches were busy trying to overtake the population; and their efforts were being rewarded with success. At the time of the American Revolution, only about one person in twenty-five was a church member. From 1800 to 1850 the population of the land grew over four times as large, but the Churches did even better, for their membership increased twelve times over.

As America expanded, the cities grew more prosperous. There was more money for the Churches, and in the cities larger buildings for worship appeared along the streets. But city life also brought new problems for the Churches. Religion had to compete with other kinds of entertainment. On the frontier, there might be no relief from the monotony of life except the occasional camp meeting. In the city, however, there were cafes and beer gardens and amusement parks and saloons and theaters. There was a place for revivals amidst these worldly distractions, and evangelists began to turn their attention to the task of appealing to the city dwellers. Sensational preachers packed the halls, and the crowds joined in the catchy religious songs they loved.

"Winning souls," as the preachers called it, was the chief aim. But there were evils to fight by other means besides revivals. Crusades were declared against everything that religious folk thought harmful. The Churches had led in the fight against slavery. They fought now against alcohol, sometimes against dancing, against tobacco. Some even fought the drinking of tea and coffee.

Whether in the country or in the city, America had discovered a new, free life. There were strange new frontiers in mining camps, on ranches, on farms, on dusty streets. And wherever any frontier called to men, the Churches followed. They had a duty to do, and nothing would turn them back.

There were farther frontiers than those of the American continent. There were other continents, and islands in the distant seas. The businessmen of Europe were reaping a harvest of wealth from trade in all corners of the world. Trading companies were growing rich—often at the expense of native peoples in Asia and in Africa, caring more about money than about men's lives. But the Churches cared. The Churches awoke to the fact that there were souls to save in heathen lands.

It had been the Roman Catholics, not the Protestants, who took the lead in missions at the time of the Reformation. A larger opportunity was open to them, for it was nations of the Roman Catholic faith—France, Spain, Portugal—that then held the overseas settlements and controlled the oceans. No peril daunted the spirits of their heroic missionaries, who made their way into savage and dangerous places to plant their Church eventually across the whole globe. They thought it a privilege to die, in order to take their faith into China, Japan, Eastern Asia, India, Africa, the South Sea Islands. Jesuit missionaries in Canada died in horrible tortures, at the hands of the Indians they came to save. In Canada too Roman Catholic settlers from France occupied what became the province of Quebec, planting a large colony, loyal to their Church and their own French-Canadian customs, in the midst of the country.

Protestants were slower to see the opportunity. But for missions to the North American Indians, they had at first taken little interest in spreading their faith among other peoples. In the eighteenth century, however, the Protestant Churches awoke to the challenge of distant lands. The stirring of new religious life in Germany, through the pietist movement, inspired a number of missionaries to go abroad from that land. From other European countries too, volunteers set out for foreign fields. Soon, however, Britain and America surpassed all other nations in the organizing of missions throughout the world.

In England, it was a young Baptist minister named William Carey, who earned his living as a shoemaker and studied while he worked at his trade, that helped to lead the way across the sea. His pleas at first fell on deaf ears.

In vain, at the beginning, did he urge that it was the duty of the Church to send the gospel to the heathen. "Young man," said someone at a meeting where Carey spoke, "when God intends to save the heathen he will do it without your help or mine!"

But the Church could not forever hide from the challenge. The missionary mood was growing. In 1792, the Baptist Missionary Society was founded, and Carey sailed to India as its first representative. Later, Churches would support their missionaries. Carey had to support himself, which at first he did by managing a dye factory in order to save his family from starvation. Under the strain his wife lost her mind. But Carey persisted; he would not forsake the work to which he had put his hand. A brilliant student of languages, he translated the

Bible into several of the native tongues spoken in India, for he knew that the Bible is the best missionary. Later he was made a professor in Calcutta; and in that position he continued to work for the mission he had built. His influence grew, and at his suggestion some of the evils of his adopted land were ended. In 1799 he had been shocked to see a widow burned alive beside the corpse of her dead husband, her tormented body held in the flames by bamboo poles. She was only one of many. In that part of India then ruled by Britain, a thousand widows yearly lost their lives through this cruel and ancient custom. In 1829 Carey persuaded the governor-general to forbid this practice in British India.

Other denominations were not long in following the example of Carey and his Church. It was slow work for the brave and patient pioneers. Carey waited seven years before he won a single convert.

In Burma, the American missionary Adoniram Judson waited six years. Judson was the first Protestant missionary from America to go outside the Western Hemisphere to plant a new Church. His sufferings, his leadership, and his example made a great impression at home: such a man could not be left to stand alone, and soon reinforcements were sent to his side. After so slow and painful a beginning, a strong Church grew up in Burma.

Robert Morrison, sent out to China from London, also labored seven long years before he persuaded anyone to become a Christian. It was especially discouraging for Morrison, for the Chinese were suspicious of foreigners and would give no help in studying their language. It was the aim of the Chinese government to prevent outsiders— "barbarians," they called them—from coming into contact with their own people; and printing the Bible or trying to spread the Christian faith was made a crime punishable by death. Yet Morrison both translated the Bible and distributed it, and laid the foundation for a Christian Church in days to come.

There were many others. There was, for one, John Coleridge Patteson. He was an Anglican clergyman, the son of a British judge, who knew himself called by God to go to the South Sea Islands. Almost his first duty there was to bury two Presbyterian missionaries from Canada, whom the natives had murdered; and later Patteson himself was slain. There were Robert Moffat and David Livingstone of Scotland, who opened up the unexplored jungles of Africa. There were too many to name: but all the Churches played their part, and missionaries forsook the comforts of home and sometimes laid down their lives. Before the century was over, Protestant congregations had been planted all across the face of the globe. Some met in mud huts, some in private homes, some in the open air. Converts were often baptized in running streams nearby. Some congregations were composed of savages and former cannibals, some of civilized Chinese and Indians. The Church no longer belonged to Europe and America alone. The Church belonged to all the world.

It was discouraging at first; yet the missionaries had advantages too. In the English-speaking world there was more wealth than ever before—money enough to pay for missions if Christians would only rise to their opportunity. In the years following 1815 no great wars convulsed the world; and in the long reign of peace, broken only by small conflicts, missionary work went on without much interruption. Governments and trading companies had opened up the far regions of the earth; and under their protection missionaries oftentimes found safety. This kind of safety had its drawbacks, however, for the cruelty of those who went abroad to trade gave the native peoples a low opinion of the so-called "Christian" nations and the religion in which they claimed to believe. There was a vast difference between what missionaries preached and what traders and government officials practiced. But, on the other hand. the machinery and medicine and education that Europe and America had brought were very welcome. There was something to be said for Christianity after all, men thought, if it had produced the wonders of modern science!

It was, on the whole, a good time for missions; the prospects were bright. The Churches streamed across the far frontiers of the earth. Some Christians grew very optimistic, and declared they were out to win the whole world to Christ in one generation. The time had come, they said, to carry out Christ's command: "Go ye into all the world, and preach the gospel to every creature."

Then there were frontiers of new thoughts and new ideas. These also the Churches must cross. But there was a feeling of danger here—more than among cannibals, more than in foreign nations. The Churches might hope to win the far places of the earth for Christ. But what, meantime, was happening at home?

Men were winning liberty—liberty to vote, to worship as they chose, to think what they liked, to say what they believed. The old order was breaking up—and there were some who were afraid. In the Church of England, a little group of men at Oxford began to plead for the glories of the distant past. They exalted the Church, with its age-old history, its ancient doctrines, its lovely ritual. The Christian leaders of the day had been appealing to individuals to accept Christ, each for himself. Let men think rather of the Church as a whole, of the Church as it has always been in days gone by: that was the message and the plea of the Oxford writers. The most famous of their group, John Henry Newman, went all the way that his beliefs were leading him, and forsook the Church of England altogether. Later he was made a cardinal of the Roman Catholic Church. Most of the others stayed with the Church of England, and within that denomination set up a way of thought and worship that was called "Anglo-Catholic." Even outside that Church they made their influence felt, helping to revive an interest in the history of the Church and to awaken a taste for better hymns and nobler church architecture.

But most men could not find much comfort or much guidance in a study of the ancient past. There were too many present-day problems that had to be faced. Did men need religion in the world of modern science? It was clear that many no longer wanted it. The earth was being conquered by trains and steamboats, by the telegraph, by the telephone. It was a great triumph of human reason. Man was mastering the world he lived in. Did he any longer need the help of God?

The question went even deeper than that. Geologists were discovering the rock formations of the earth. How, they asked, could the story of creation in Genesis be true, when fossils seemed to prove that the earth was so much older than the Bible said? Then arose the theory that animals and birds and men, and all living creatures, were not created at one time or in six days. It was claimed that one form of life developed into another, by a process of evolution, and that man himself was descended from the lower animals. This theory came as a shock to Christian ears. was man not, after all, made in the image of God, as the Scriptures taught?

One way, and then another, was tried to meet the challenge. Some said that science, rightly understood, really proved the Bible right. Others said flatly that science was wrong, and must never be believed when it contradicted Scripture. Still others claimed that science had its own place, in the physical world, while religion was a matter of morals and spiritual values with which science could not interfere. Some declared that evolution was God's noble way of carrying on his creative work: it showed that God is always busy developing the world into something better than before.

For a great many, it simply became a contest between science and the Bible; or between what they called "the new" and "the old." But science was beginning to trouble the reader of the Bible in other ways as well. For scholars were coming to the conclusion that the Bible had to be read like any other book. It was not, they said, dictated by God, without any error. Human beings wrote it. It was the literature of an ancient people, in many ways like the literature of other nations of old time. one had to know the history of the ages in which the various books were written: then one could understand both the values and the errors of the Scripture.

It came as a surprise to be told that Moses did not write the first five books of the Old Testament; that there were at least two writers, centuries apart, who composed the book of Isaiah; that John was not so accurate an account of Jesus' life as was Mark. There were scholars who went so far as to state that there was very little truth in any of the stories about Jesus; that the gospel was mainly a myth. Others were less extreme. They assured Christians that there really was a person named Jesus of Nazareth, and that a great deal written about him in the New Testament was true: but it still took study and science to discover what was correct and what was not.

A great controversy over the "higher criticism," as it was called, broke out in the Churches. Many welcomed the new scholarship. It would, they said, eventually shed more light on the Bible than Christians had ever had before. Besides, they claimed for themselves and others the right to believe and teach what they held to be the truth. Others were hostile. Ministers and professors were accused of heresy, and some lost their posts. Everyone was confused. It sometimes seemed as though the very foundations of the Church were being shaken. What could a person believe in any more?

The frontiers of new thought proved hard and rocky. The Church did not know whether it could safely cross them; whether it was safe to think these problems out or better to hold to old beliefs as if science and the new teachings had never been heard of. The Church had met modern science—and hardly knew whether to fight, stand still, or flee.

There were other frontiers besides. The consciences of Christians were troubled by the lot of the poor, by the ruthlessness of the rich and powerful, by the cruelty of prisons, by the horrors of war. Doubt may have been cast upon the ancient Christian faith, but on one point many churchmen could have no doubt, and that was as to their Christian duty to reform the world.

Here science might even be a help and not a hindrance. With the powers opened up by man's discoveries, surely the world could be better than ever before. Science might help to build the Kingdom of God! But whether they looked for the aid of scientists or not, many were the Christian preachers who were loud in denouncing the wrongs they saw about them every day. They preached what they called "the social gospel"—the gospel of social reform.

There was pity for the weak, and there was anger toward those who took advantage of them. Also there was a great hope. The world did seem to be growing better. Why should it not continue to improve? Enlightened people were turning away from cruelty, from oppression, from bloodshed, from indifference toward the sufferings of others. The conscience could no longer stand idly by and watch the few get rich at the expense of the many. Besides, there were more of the good things of life available for everyone—for everyone in America at any rate, except the most destitute and unfortunate. Perhaps even the poorest could at last gain their share of this world's blessings.

> These things shall be: a loftier race
> Than e'er the world hath known shall rise....
> Nation with nation, land with land,
> Unarmed shall live as comrades free.

So they sang, and so they dreamed. War would be banished soon. Perhaps already the world was too civilized to support another war.

In 1914, to the amazement and the grief of all who hoped that peace had come to stay, the World War broke out. It promised to be the greatest war the world had ever known—surely the greatest it would ever know! But there was at least this consolation: it would be the last one. This would be, men said, "the war to end war." The horrible deeds that the enemy were said to have done would never again be committed. The sacrifice would be immense; but it would be worth it to "make the world safe for democracy." Let this war only be won, and then there really would be peace at last, peace to be broken nevermore!

The world was crossing another frontier—over into a new age. And as men crossed, amidst blood and mud and gunfire, across the dreadful stretches of no man's land, Christians believed that "the blessed Kingdom of the Right" lay straight ahead.

CHAPTER 18

MIDNIGHT HOUR

TEN million men were killed, and twenty-one million wounded. But in 1918 the victory was won: the nations of the world need never fight again. Mixed with prayers of thankfulness were noble hopes—hopes that men would now follow the ideals that so many of the brave had died for. *It must not happen again*, the Churches said. A League of Nations would guard the peace of the world, and settle disputes without violence or bloodshed. Men would be free and happy, as they had never been before.

But not everyone was thinking about ideals. Four precious years had been lost from the lives of those who survived the long and weary war. Many were longing, not for a new world, but for the old world they had known before the armies had to march away. They wanted to live now as though nothing had been changed. They did not see as yet that nothing could ever be the same again.

Certainly things would not be the same in Russia. Everyone who could read the newspapers knew that there was trouble there. Russia had not seen the war through to the end. Instead, it had had a revolution. The Government had been overthrown, the Bolsheviks had taken power, and it looked as though the Church, along with the Government, must perish. In western Europe, and especially in America, men heard the news from Russia with alarm.

Until now, not many had given much thought to Russia or its Church. After the barbarians overran Europe in the early centuries, the Church in the East had gone its own way. Safe under the protection of the Empire, with its capital at Constantinople, the Eastern Church had been under the thumb of the men who still bore the title of "Caesar." The faith spread northward, and in 988 Russia officially became Christian. A few centuries later, Constantinople was taken by the Moslems. Russia had already gained its independence, and now the Church of that country was independent too. The ruler of Russia, the czar, began to call himself the successor of Caesar; and the Russian Church, now free of the old Empire, became one of the members of that band of Churches which together went by the name of Greek Orthodox. But the Russian Church was not free from the czar. In 1721, Czar Peter the Great, to make sure that the Church would always be under his control, founded the Holy Synod. This was a group of bishops, who ruled the Church; but they in turn took their orders from the czar, who declared that he was "the guardian of true faith and of the welfare of the Holy Church."

The Eastern Church was different from that of the West. To the outsider its worship was weird and strange, but to its own people it was rich and precious, full of pageantry and color. There was nothing elsewhere like the night of Easter in the Orthodox Church. Before midnight, the worshipers would gather in the church to bid farewell to the image of the dead Christ, which was to be carried away. At midnight the bells rang, and a hymn burst out: "The angels sing in heaven thy resurrection, O Savior Christ." Then priests, carrying lights, walked forth among a multitude of people with candles in their hands. As the bells continued to ring, the procession marched three times around the outside of the church, and stopped before the closed doors, which stood for the sealed tomb of Christ. The doors swung open, and the priests entered, chanting victoriously, "Christ is risen from the dead!" All the worshipers would then break out in expressions of joy and gaiety. It was to them as though Christ had just risen again in that very place.

Religion was deep and rich for the faithful of the Church. But Russia was very poor, and men without enough land to earn a living looked jealously on the great estates of the monasteries. Those who longed for a new day in Russia linked the Church together with the Government, for the Church was the tool of the Government, forced to do the bidding of the czar. Revolutionary ideas had long been seeping into the country, and many of the leaders of the new thought were atheists. They got their chance to overthrow the old way of life in 1917. Russia had suffered terribly from the war, and the masses of the people never understood what it was about. Food was short in the cities. The Communists promised what millions were longing for—peace, food, land, freedom. They struck at the right moment: the Government toppled, and with it fell the Church.

Under the new Communist Government people were still free to worship—but not to spread the Christian faith. They could go to church, but to gather large numbers of children together to instruct them in Christianity was forbidden. Meanwhile the new- schools were teaching the young to despise religion. Many of the religious leaders had to Bee from the country. Some who remained were for one reason or another jailed. Still the worshipers gathered by the thousand for the ancient ceremonies, but at enormous cost. The best jobs were not open to Christians; and the priests must live on what little their supporters could spare them from their own small resources. At one village service a visitor counted the offering. It was not in money, for no one had enough money to give. It consisted of five pieces of black bread, four green apples, and one egg.

The sincere and the steadfast still stood by; they did not forsake their Church. But the Church as a whole in Russia had to suffer—the innocent along with the guilty—because for so many long centuries gone by a Government that called itself Christian had failed to care about the needs of men. And millions who had been hungry were glad enough to give up the feast of the Resurrection, when they saw tractors bringing food from the dead soil; and those who had never known anything but want were ready to trade the Holy Communion for the goods they could buy from Communist shops.

The people of the democracies were disturbed by what was happening in Russia. Not only the downfall of the Church alarmed them, but the loss of men's property, the end of a way of life in which a man was free to make a fortune. A wave of fear swept America. Could it happen here? Were there perhaps enough Communists in this land to overthrow the Government as they had done in Russia? In some places it became unpopular to preach social reform—that might be opening the door to Communism. Yet the Churches persisted in demanding that Christian countries should rid themselves of evils. Church leaders talked about the brotherhood of man, about doing away with differences between nations and races and classes, above all about peace.

Some listened, but many did not greatly care. There were other things to think about besides religion or "the good life." Every person could hope to have an automobile, a radio. For entertainment there were the movies. The talk of America was the first solo flight across the ocean or the number of home runs that a baseball star had scored.

There still were plenty of people in the Churches, but many no longer knew what they believed. It became fashionable to say that it did not matter what a man's religion was, so long as he was sincere. All the religions of the world, some said, were simply different ways of finding God. The Bible was just another book of religion—noble in places, but not always equal to the highest standards that men have discovered through the ages. The Church was an organization for doing good works in the neighborhood, not a fellowship of believers who

178

lived by their faith in Jesus Christ. Jesus himself was the greatest teacher and the best man who ever lived—and nothing more. The heart of Christianity was nothing more or less than the Golden Rule.

Other voices, however, were beginning to speak. They spoke most clearly in Europe, but in Britain and in America too. They declared that God is known only through his Son Jesus Christ; and that he speaks through the Bible and the preaching of the Church. They stated that a Church without a living faith in Christ is not true to itself. They insisted that men must listen to the way in which *God* chooses to speak, and not be satisfied with worshiping the beauties of nature or the wonders of this world. They preached that man is a sinner, needing God's mercy, which is offered in the death and resurrection of the Lord Jesus Christ.

It was the preaching that the Church had heard from the beginning, the preaching which made the Reformation great. Yet it sounded strange to modern ears. Could anyone believe these things in the twentieth century? Could it be true, as these men said, that even though the Bible was a very human book, and even though it was not a textbook for students of science, nevertheless it was God's living Word to man?

Educated people were somewhat confused. They were even inclined to laugh a little. But they did not laugh so loudly after 1933.

In 1933, Adolf Hitler came into power in Germany. Here was another revolution! Again there was alarm—but Germany was still weak, and there surely was no chance that it could soon grow strong enough to wage another war. There was horror too when Jews were whipped and imprisoned in Germany under the Hitler Government. Yet few realized that if the Jews were persecuted today, the Christian Church would suffer tomorrow.

But Hitler had his plans laid out. The religion that had come from the Hebrews and the Christians would not have long to live. There would be a new religion in Germany—a religion of "blood, race, and soil." It would make the nation great. German youth were to be encouraged to worship the mysteries in nature, not the God and Father of Jesus Christ. Let them look for inspiration to the starry heavens, the snow upon the ground, the buds and birds returning in the springtime of the year. Above all, let them rejoice in the blood in their veins—good northern blood, German blood, infinitely better than that of inferior tribes or races! Let them sing:

A thousand years before thee
have guarded thy blood,
that thou becamest just
what thou art.

Guard thy blood, that
the generations that come
a thousand years after thee
have cause to thank thee!

For those who still clung to Christianity, there would be a Church; but the Government would decide what that Church would teach and how it should be managed. It would be a *German* Church above all; and in nothing would it believe, preach, or act against the interests of the German nation. It would even go so far as to say: "Through Hitler Christ, God the Helper and Redeemer, has become mighty amongst us." Its faith would be: "Because we believe in God, we believe in Germany."

There were Germans who could not bow the knee to the new Government or the new religion. At Barmen, in May, 1934, representatives of the Churches met to proclaim their faith. They saw clearly what was happening. The nation was swallowing up the total life of its people; it had become "totalitarian." And it was able to do this because the Churches had forsaken their loyalty to Christ as their one Lord in life and death. When the Church grew careless, paganism came in the door. In language that no one could mistake, the ministers at Barmen declared that there is no way of knowing God except through his Son Jesus Christ; and that no human being, no earthly leader or dictator, could take his place. To him—to him alone— the Church owes obedience.

The Government knew what they meant. Some of those who put themselves on the side of the ministers went to jail, to concentration camps. Some were never heard of again. Others lived daily in fear of their lives. But they stood fast. For they knew the commandment: "I am the Lord thy God, . . . thou shalt have no other gods before me."

Outside of Germany, what had happened at Barmen was not widely known. But five years later the whole world knew where Hitlerism was leading. In 1939, all the prayers and hopes for peace had to be laid aside. A power was loose in Europe that must be chained, if men were to sleep quietly in their beds at night.

In 1939, twenty-five years after the First World War began, the second exploded. It was worse even than men had feared. It did not end until atomic bombs fell on the Japanese cities of Hiroshima and Nagasaki—killing over a hundred thousand persons in those unhappy places, and filling mankind with terror of what a third world war might hold.

In August, 1948, about 350 persons, from approximately 150 branches of the Christian Church, met in Amsterdam. They had gathered from all parts of the earth for the Assembly of the World Council of Churches. They represented 175,000,000 Christians scattered throughout the world.

There were men from America, from the British Commonwealth, from France. There were Germans and Danes and Norwegians and Swedes—some of them heroes who had valiantly withstood the Hitler forces in the war. Many countries of the Old World were present through their delegates; and also the "younger Churches" of Asia and Africa and the South Sea Islands. A Canadian would chat with an Abyssinian on the streetcar; a minister from Switzerland with one from Formosa. Christian leaders from many different nations were the speakers. The same hymns were sung at once in English, French, and German.

But there were some Churches that were not there. The 175,000,000 Christians represented were not all the Christians in the world. The Roman Catholic Church had no one present. And the Orthodox Church of Russia, behind the "iron curtain," could send no one to speak for it.

Amsterdam is a city of bridges and canals and ancient buildings. To the stranger it also seemed a city of many clocks—forever publicly chiming the hour of the day. Some wondered what hour they were striking. Was it midnight —the midnight of ruin and despair? There was reason to think so. There was no one there without his fears. Dark and barbarous times seemed to loom ahead, casting their shadows on everybody's heart. The old, familiar world was breaking up, and nobody knew what the future was going to bring. It might bring war—war between Russia and the Western world, the third world war in one generation. It might bring the end of civilization as mankind had known it. No one could tell.

Or the clocks might be striking the hour of early dawn. For the world was not unlike what it had been when Christianity first began. The Church was having to fight its own battles, by the power of faith alone. In some countries of Europe it was already being put to the test, and persecution might grow worse. Where it was not persecuted, it was oftentimes despised. By the strength of God, then, it would advance! It was as though the Church were beginning anew. Believing, it would conquer as before.

What was going to become of the Church would not be settled at Amsterdam. The delegates were there only to listen and discuss, and perhaps also lead the way. The future of the Church would be decided in the sermons preached Sunday by Sunday in congregations across the face of the earth, in the prayers of millions, in the faith and life of the people who called themselves by the name of Christ. But this Assembly might accomplish something.

The delegates could find there a sense that all nations now belong to one world: a small world, full of people with very much the same hopes and the same fears. They could believe that "the God of the West is also God of the East." They could discover that there are more things uniting the Churches of the world than need to divide them. They could rid themselves of prejudices that separate Christian from Christian. They could feel in one another, from the greatest to the least, humility before God, who alone can save mankind. They could sense one another's loyalty to Christ, the only Lord. They could see that the cause of the world's great troubles is that "man has lost his Lord," and does not know where to go or what to do. They could hear again the gospel of the power of God, which raises the dead and gives life to human souls. They could face together the needs of men, and believe together in the might and mercy of their God.

They could not agree on all things, nor could they an see clearly. But they could share their faith in the divine Lord, Jesus Christ. They could know that neither America nor Russia nor any other nation is going to save the world. They could *hope*— and their hope would be in no human power, but in Christ, the world's Redeemer. To him be the victory, and the power, and the glory—even "to the close of the age"!

The clocks struck again. It was surely midnight they were striking—the mysterious hour of darkness, when one day ends and another day is born.